The ACADIAN KITCHEN

ALAIN BOSSÉ *The Kilted Chef*

The ACADIAN KITCHEN

RECIPES *from* THEN *and* NOW

whitecap

Whitecap Books is known for its expertise in the cookbook market, and has produced some of the most innova-
tive and familiar titles found in kitchens across North America. Visit our website at www.whitecap.ca.

EDITOR Patrick Geraghty
DESIGN Andrew Bagatella
PHOTOGRAPHY Perry Jackson

Additional contributions to the text by Joseph Muise. Additional photography pages vi,
xii, xv, 6, 9, 14, 50, 51, 56, 62, 66, 85, 94, 101, 124, 129, 131, 132, 141, 158, 159, 172, 179, and 297
by Alain Bossé; vi, x, 14, 18, 19, 20, 23, 24, 36, 93, and 228 by Mike Hall; 44, 146, 156,
and 208 by Linda Duncan; 72 by Alcide Bernard

Library and Archives Canada Cataloguing in Publication

Bossé, Alain, 1964-, author
The Acadian kitchen : recipes from then and now / Alain Bossé.

Includes index. ISBN 978-1-77050-313-7 (softcover)

1. Cooking, Acadian. 2. Cooking, Acadian--History. 3. Cookbooks. I. Title.

TX715.6.B67 2018   641.59715   C2017-908080-6

We acknowledge the financial support of the Government of Canada through the Canada Book Fund (CBF) for
our publishing activities and the Province of British Columbia through the Book Publishing Tax Credit.

Nous reconnaissons l'appui financier du gouvernement du Canada et la province de la
Colombie-Britannique par le Book Publishing Tax Credit.

Printed in China

18 19 20 21 22 23   6 5 4 3 2 1

DEDICATION

I'VE BEEN FORTUNATE to have been surrounded by some very strong people during my lifetime, people who had a huge influence on me and who have shaped me into the person I am today. I was a "later in life baby" and as a result I grew up with four mothers—my mom Carmen, my older sisters Marjolaine and Lyne, and my sister-in-law Monique. There was no shortage of love and certainly no shortage of advice, and whether it was sought after or came unsolicited it was more often than not right. I can't thank them enough for their guidance and support. I hope they feel that their investment has paid off!

There were two other men with me in this passel of women: my dad Leonard, who left us much too soon, and my brother Yves who stepped in to fill the void. Some days he played the role of father and other times he was all big brother—lending me a cool car, giving me refuge from the women at home, and covering for me when I did something the women would definitely not have approved of! Your guidance and wisdom have never fallen on deaf ears. Never doubt your contribution to my success.

And just when I thought there wasn't room for another independent, stubborn, strong-willed woman, another came along! My wife Johanne. You challenge me to the point where I think I've reached my creative limit then you push me a little further. Your constant reminder that "good enough will never be good enough" keeps me on my toes and makes me want to do better. I know this isn't the life you envisioned, but I can't envision this life with anyone else. Merci mon petit chou.

To you all, thank you.

—*Alain*

TABLE OF CONTENTS

FOREWORD

I MET ALAIN a few years ago when we were both participating in one of Canada's coveted chef competitions at the PEI Shellfish Festival in Prince Edward Island where Alain was the Master of Ceremonies. Having heard him work the crowd and interact with competitors from Canada and the USA, it was evident that here was one of the culinary stars of Atlantic Canada. Alain loves to teach and he was a master at translating the activities and ingredients from a commercial kitchen to the consumer's home.

The Acadian Kitchen takes Chef Alain's passion for the Acadian culture he grew up in and its food and showcases it in an insightful cookbook full of amazing flavours and features. He presents numerous recipes from the past four centuries of Acadian cooking, as well as lots of his own pleasing creations, and makes them accessible through his own uncomplicated, straightforward cooking style.

This cookbook's iconic flavours bring to mind experiences of home, tradition and family, while introducing us to new ideas and ingredients. I enjoyed its historical account of the Acadians, charting how they lived and the foods that were available to them, and I highly recommend you spend some time exploring the Acadian food glossary, which I have never seen captured previously. The Acadians adapted their own recipes to the ingredients that were available to them, and a chapter following the Acadians to Louisiana and examining their influence on Cajun cooking provides a wonderful collection of interesting and delicious Cajun recipes.

I particularly like the fact that *The Acadian Kitchen* highlights cultural dishes that have deep roots in supporting local farmers and producers with the use of seasonal fresh ingredients. Chef Alain has been an ambassador of the Eat Local faction for many years, and his passion is readily on display here.

If you seek recipes that you will enjoy cooking, with insightful information about Acadian history, the exciting dishes in this book are definitely for you!

CHEF *Lynn Crawford*

PREFACE

THIS BOOK WAS born out of a passion for a culture so big and so robust that trying to contain it in the pages of a book seems like trying to capture a hurricane in a bottle. When you are surrounded by a group of Acadians you feel a palpable sense of pride, a fierce loyalty to one another, a joy and zest for life that wraps itself around you, welcomes you in, draws you close and says "you're one of us now."

This book was written because our Acadian ancestors refused to turn into a lost culture. It's true they had lost much, but they adapted—or rather, they thrived—in their new homes, and as a method of preservation they passed down their stories. Intermingled with those stories were recipes, recipes that identified them and linked them to their former home.

I grew up in a home where traditional Acadian foods were prepared. While my friends were having pasta I was having fricot, and when they had meatloaf I had chiard. Oh, how I wished my mom could cook! It wasn't until later in life, after I had become a Chef, that I truly developed an appreciation for what my mother had created for her family. Now, those recipes have become a cornerstone of my career.

The recipes in this book are not meant to be viewed as "the best fricot recipe" or "the best rappie pie recipe," because every community prepares these foods differently and every community feels that theirs is the best—and rightfully so! This book is simply a way to honour our Acadian grandmothers, yours and mine, to thank them for their efforts in keeping our traditions alive through food, for not just feeding our hunger but for feeding our minds, for teaching us what it means to be Acadian. And whether yours was a "Ma Mère" in Chetticamp or a Maw Maw in Louisiana, these women deserve much recognition and gratitude for making the culture what it is today: vibrant, strong, and alive.

ACADIAN HISTORICAL TIMELINE

1604 French settlers attempt the first Acadian settlement on Saint Croix Island, near the border between modern-day New Brunswick and Maine.

1605 The settlement is relocated to the mainland and rebuilt according to the original plan at Port-Royal.

1613–1710 Acadie changes hands between the French and British nine times.

1632–1653 Most of the French colonists that will populate Acadie arrive.

1713 The Treaty of Utrecht cedes control of Acadie to the British permanently.

1749 Halifax is founded to solidify the British presence in Nova Scotia.

1755 Lieutenant Governor Charles Lawrence orders the Deportation of the Acadians from Nova Scotia.

1755–1763 Between 10,000 and 18,000 Acadians are deported to the Anglo-American colonies, Quebec, Britain, and France in what was known as *Le Grand Dérangement* or The Great Upheaval.

1763 The Treaty of Paris cedes most of France's colonial possessions in North America to Britain.

1764 Permission is granted for Acadians to return to Nova Scotia on the condition that they swear an oath of allegiance and settle in small groups. Many return and settle in more remote areas of the colony.

1765–1785 More than 3,000 Acadians who were supposed to be deported to France made their way to the Spanish colony of Louisiana, and settled in the area upriver from New Orleans.

1847   Acadians establish their first higher education institution, Collège Saint-Joseph, in Memramcook, New Brunswick.

1867   The British North American Act unites the colonies of Nova Scotia, New Brunswick, and the province of Canada (much of present-day Ontario and Quebec) to form the Dominion of Canada.

1881   The first Acadian National Convention is held in Memramcook, New Brunswick, and August 15 is established as the Acadians' national holiday.

1884   An Acadian flag and national anthem, "Ave Maris Stella," are adopted during the second Acadian National Convention.

1890   Collège Sainte-Anne (now Université Sainte-Anne) is founded in Church Point, Nova Scotia.

1922   A commemorative church to honour the historical Acadian presence in the area is built at Grand-Pré, Nova Scotia.

1963   The Université de Moncton is established, forming what will become the largest Canadian French-language university outside of Quebec.

1994   The first Congrès Mondial Acadien (World Acadian Congress) is held in southeastern New Brunswick.

2003   A Royal Proclamation is issued by the Queen's representative in Canada, Governor General Adrienne Clarkson, recognizing the wrongs suffered by the Acadians during the Deportation, and establishing July 28 as the Day of Commemoration of the Great Upheaval.

2012   The landscape of Grand-Pré, including the commemorative church, is declared a UNESCO World Heritage Site.

INTRODUCTION

A BRIEF HISTORY OF ACADIE AND THE ACADIANS

ACADIANS ARE THE descendants of French colonists who settled a part of New France known as Acadie, in what is now Canada's East Coast. As the colony developed, a distinct Acadian culture and cuisine emerged that has survived to this day, shaped by the landscapes of the colonists' new home, their contact with Indigenous peoples and other cultures, through trade, and as a result of historical events. Due to its strategic location, Acadie was prone to invasions, and control of the colony exchanged hands between the French and the British many times during its first 150 years, a power struggle that culminated in the expulsion of large numbers of Acadians from their homeland to the New England colonies and beyond in 1755. Although some Acadians eventually returned to the region, some also settled in new areas, such as Louisiana, bringing their culinary traditions with them. Today, Acadian cuisine is still passed on from generation to generation in the various parts of the world where the Acadians settled, and it continues to evolve and incorporate new influences to this day.

FOUNDING AND COLONIZATION OF ACADIE The French colony of Acadie made up a territory that included much of modern-day Nova Scotia, Prince Edward Island, New Brunswick, and parts of the US state of Maine. The first group of settlers set sail from the French port of Le Havre in 1604 and established a settlement on Saint Croix Island in the Bay of Fundy, or *Baie Française* as it was then known, near the New Brunswick–Maine border. After a harsh winter where many emigrants were lost to scurvy, the settlement was relocated to the mainland in what is now the Annapolis Valley in Nova Scotia.

Subsequent migrations took place from 1632 to 1653, during which time most of the settlers who would populate the colony arrived. Little is known of the passengers who travelled on these ships, with the exception of the *Saint-Jehan*, which sailed from La Rochelle to Acadie in 1636 with 78 passengers on board. We know from the passenger list that these migrants included women and children, farmers, and skilled craftspeople—a cooper, a cobbler, nine carpenters, a master gardener, a gunsmith, a locksmith, four tailors, a tool-maker, a vintner, and an expert in the construction of mills. This range of skilled tradespeople speaks to France's ambitions for the colony and the desire to see it succeed as a commercial venture.

The Acadians were somewhat unique as far as French colonies in North America go, in that they were a relatively homogenous group in origin, particularly when compared to the settlements in Quebec. More than half of the settlers came from the provinces of Western France, south of the Loire River (Poitou, Aunis, Saintonge, as well as the Basque Country). The remainder came from a variety of provinces north of the Loire, including Anjou, Touraine, Brittany, Normandy, Brie, and the Orléanais.

ORIGIN OF THE NAME ACADIE The name Acadie is believed to have originated with the Italian explorer Giovanni Verrazano, who was commissioned by France to explore North America in the 16th century. Verrazano was so struck by the lush virgin forest he encountered along the Atlantic coast of North America that he called the territory "Arcadia," after the region of Ancient Greece depicted in literature as an unspoilt paradise where people lived in harmony with nature. The R was eventually dropped and we were left with "Acadie." Another theory is that the word derived from the Mi'kmaq word *algatig*, which means "a camp site," or *quoddy*, which means "fertile ground." French fishermen in the area might have mistaken these words for the name of the territory and pronounced them in their own way as "Acadie." Whatever the origin, by 1603 the region was being referred to as "Acadie" or "La Cadie" in the official documents of King Henri IV of France and in the writings of Samuel de Champlain, the King's cartographer.

GROWTH AND DEVELOPMENT OF THE ACADIAN COLONY From the initial settlement at Port-Royal, new communities would begin to take root in the area surrounding the Bay of Fundy. The most significant of these were at Grand-Pré in the Minas Basin area of the Annapolis Valley, which would become the largest Acadian settlement, and at Beaubassin on the Isthmus of Chignecto, near modern-day Amherst, Nova Scotia. There were also smaller communities at Cape Sable (on the southwest tip of the Nova Scotian peninsula), Île-Royale (Cape Breton), Isle Saint-Jean (Prince Edward Island), and along the St. John River, among others. The Acadian population grew from a few hundred in 1671 to more than 2,500 by 1714. By 1755, there were an estimated 12,000 to 20,000 Acadians living in various parts of what would become the Maritime Provinces. Though small numbers of immigrants did make their way to Acadie during this period, the rapid population growth was mostly due to the high fertility and low mortality rates of the Acadians.

ACADIAN FARMING AND FORAGING The Acadian colony took an unusual approach to farming that was unique in North America at the time. Rather than

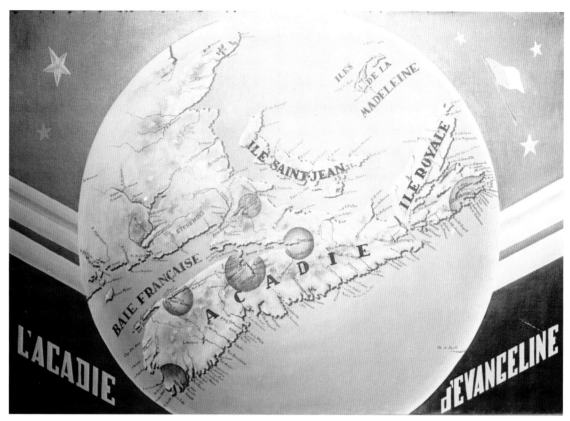

TOP French Acadian map of Nova Scotia, Prince Edward Island, and New Brunswick (year unknown); **BOTTOM LEFT** Mrs. Marie Doucette churning butter, 1950; **BOTTOM RIGHT** Acadian woman, 1856, wearing a bonnet typical of the time. (All images courtesy of Nova Scotia Archives.)

clearing the uplands to plant crops, as was typical in other colonial settlements, the Acadians constructed a system of dykes to reclaim marshlands along the shoreline. This was achieved by placing a small wooden conduit known as an *aboiteau* at the base of the embankment of the dykes, through which excess fresh water could flow out to sea. A small door known as a *clapet* prevented the salt water from flowing into the marshlands at high tide.

This technique proved very successful. The rich clay soils were extremely fertile and resulted in exceptional yields for Acadian farmers. Indeed, yields were as much as twice those achievable in the parts of France from which the settlers came. The fertility of the soil also meant that they did not have to leave the land fallow to replenish the soil, as was the custom elsewhere.

Acadians planted a number of crops, including wheat, oats, buckwheat, peas, and flax, mainly for their own consumption. They also planted apple orchards and tended to vegetable gardens. They raised livestock for meat and milk, as well as for sale in what appears to have been a booming trade. In fact, by 1707, when the Acadian population numbered some 1800, there were more cattle, sheep, and pigs than people, and livestock were undoubtedly one of the colony's main exports. Pigs were reared for their meat, while cows were used mainly for their milk. The Acadians kept chickens for eggs and meat, as well as sheep, which were used as a source of wool.

Acadians foraged for wild plants and berries, which they called *grainage*, in and around their settlements. Berries such as cranberries and *pommes de pré* (literally "meadow apples"), blueberries, wild strawberries, and blackberries were picked and transformed into jams and preserves. Several varieties of wild herbs, such as *anise* (a type of caraway), summer savory, and greens including wild spinach and dandelion leaves were also used in Acadian cooking. Acadians consumed a variety of wild Jerusalem artichoke, which they called *topinambour*, that grew in the areas where they lived. Contact with Indigenous tribes introduced new foods to the Acadian diet, such as corn, which was not consumed in France at the time. Acadians also learned to make maple syrup and maple sugar from the sap of maple trees.

The early Acadians did not appear to have been trappers or hunters. Remains of the houses excavated at the Acadian settlement at Belleisle contained few traces of bones from anything but domestic livestock, including cows, pigs, sheep, and poultry. Of the few bones from wild species that were uncovered, we find game birds such as passenger pigeon and goose, as well as hare. The early Acadians most certainly caught and ate fish (both salted and fresh), in accordance with Catholic tradition, as well as the shellfish that was abundant in the area.

DOMESTIC LIFE IN EARLY ACADIE The success of Acadian agriculture meant that years of famine and low yields were relatively infrequent. Although there is very little in the way of contemporary accounts of the homes and domestic lives of these early Acadians, recent archaeological excavations, beginning in the 1980s, have shed more light on this aspect of the Acadian experience.

In comparison to other frontier settlements of the period that mostly consisted of log cabins, Acadian homes and domestic life appear to have been unusually advanced for the time. From the archaeological evidence unearthed at the Annapolis Valley sites, we know that early Acadians lived in homes built from solid wooden beams with bright, whitewashed clay walls and thatched roofs, built up with marsh grasses from the lands they cultivated. Inside each dwelling was a large stone-and-clay hearth, which would have been used both for cooking and as a source of heat in the winter. Another unusual feature of some of these early Acadian homes was that they had outdoor bake ovens, a feature that was not found elsewhere in North America.

Acadians were not self-sufficient and traded for items that they could not produce or obtain locally, including ceramics, cooking implements, firearms, certain types of cloth, spices such as cinnamon, cloves, and nutmeg, and molasses from the West Indies. They traded with the New England colonies, with French merchant ships that visited the area, and with other French colonial settlements, such as Louisbourg. Archaeological excavations of Acadian homes unearthed tableware from England, France, and the New England colonies, as well as many examples of green earthenware. The green earthenware found at these sites was typical of that produced in the former province of Saintonge in western France, located near the port La Rochelle from which many of the passenger ships and fishing vessels headed to Acadie departed.

Acadian women played an important role in Acadian domestic life, preparing meals and taking care of household chores while the men worked in the fields or on fishing vessels. For hundreds of years, Acadian recipes were passed on from mother to daughter, one generation to the next. Within the first two generations of settling, the food and Acadian style of cooking were clearly distinct from those of their European French compatriots, as noted by visitors familiar with the cooking and traditional dishes of both regions.

THE STRUGGLE FOR CONTROL OF ACADIE For much of the first 150 years of Acadian settlement, France and England were either at war or staking claims on parts of the American continent. Due to the strategic location of the Acadian colony along the trade routes from Boston and the West Indies, as well as the colony's proximity to important fishing banks, Acadians often found themselves in the crosshairs of this larger power struggle.

Between 1604 and 1710, Acadie changed hands no fewer than nine times. This meant that at different times over this period Acadians found themselves under either British or French colonial rule. To adapt this reality, Acadians remained neutral, preferring not to take sides in the event of war or further conflict between the two European powers. Their status as "French Neutrals" was well known and they were referred to as such in letters and documents produced by the British colonial administration. In 1713, the British gained control of the colony with the signing of the Treaty of Utrecht and renamed the territory Nova Scotia.

THE DEPORTATION The most tragic period of Acadian history began in 1755, a time of rising tensions between France and Britain. On 28 July 1755, Governor Charles Lawrence passed an order to deport the "French inhabitants" from the colony of Nova Scotia. This event, which occurred over several years, became known to the Acadians as the *Le Grand Dérangement* or "The Great Upheaval." Over the next months and years, Acadians were rounded up from their settlements, loaded onto boats, and transported out of Nova Scotia, chiefly to the Anglo-American colonies along the eastern seaboard of North America. Many others were returned directly to France, and more than one thousand Acadians died on trips across the Atlantic when their transport ships sank, or they contracted diseases. Some Acadian families managed to escape into the wilderness or to remote parts of the colony to avoid deportation.

A few eventually settled in the colonies to which they had been deported, assimilating into American culture and anglicizing their surnames in the process—LeBlanc to White, Poirier to Perry—while others made their way to more familiar or more welcoming parts of the New World. Remarkably, over the course of this great migration that lasted for several years, sometimes a decade or more, many families that had been separated were reunited through a well-developed communication network of letters and verbal messages.

RETURN OF THE ACADIANS After years in exile, permission was granted for Acadians to return to Nova Scotia in 1764. Upon receiving news of the change in policy, many Acadians in the Anglo-American colonies, Quebec, and France returned. Upon returning they found that the lands they had once occupied had been taken over, and they established themselves in more remote areas of the colony.

The returning Acadians settled in the areas of the Baie Sainte-Marie and Argyle in southwestern Nova Scotia, Chéticamp and Isle Madame in Cape Breton, around Malpeque on Prince Edward Island, the St. John River Valley, and in northern and eastern parts of New Brunswick. Since the soils in the areas where they established themselves were often of poorer quality than those they had cultivated in and around Grand-Pré and Port-Royal, Acadians turned to the sea as a source of food and income. More wild game was also introduced to the Acadian diet during this period, including porcupine, deer, and moose. The return of the Acadians continued over several years and, by the beginning of the 19th century, a total of about 1600 Acadians had returned to the colony.

THE CATHOLIC CHURCH IN ACADIE Most Acadians were Catholic, and the church played an important role in their lives both before and after the Deportation. Catholic priests were among the first groups of settlers in Acadie, and missionary priests would continue to serve the Acadians returning after the Deportation until permanent parishes were established. As well as performing a religious and educational role, the Catholic clergy serving Acadian communities wielded considerable authority and were often called upon to give advice on legal and trade matters. What's more, the detailed records kept by the Catholic clergy provide some of the only written accounts of the lives of early Acadians.

NEW BEGINNINGS Many Acadians decided to settle in new areas after the Deportation. Hundreds of Acadians deported to the Anglo-American colonies made their way south to Louisiana, a former French territory that had been ceded to Spain. The French had named the territory Louisiane in honour of King Louis XIV, and between 1765 and 1785 more than three thousand Acadians who had been deported to France travelled to Louisiana. By the early 1800s, roughly a fifth of Acadians worldwide were living in the territory.

Most Louisiana-bound Acadians settled upriver from New Orleans in an area of prairies, swamps, and bayous. The administrative districts, or parishes, in this area would become known collectively as Acadiana, and their inhabitants were referred to as "Cajuns," a local corruption of the word Acadian. The Acadians adapted to life in their new surroundings, incorporating local ingredients such as okra and mirlitons (chayote squash) into their cooking and making use of the abundant fish, shellfish, and wild game (duck and rabbit) available in the region. The Cajuns managed to maintain their culture, traditions, and identity in their new home.

Large numbers of Acadians also settled in Quebec, where religious, cultural, and linguistic similarities to other French Canadians meant they could easily integrate into society. To this day, the largest population of Acadian descent is in the province of Quebec. Smaller numbers of Acadians settled in Newfoundland, France, and other French-controlled territories, including Saint-Pierre et Miquelon, Santo Domingo (Haiti), and Guyana. All these migrations contributed to the Acadian diaspora we know today.

CONTEMPORARY ACADIANS The first stirrings of a renewed Acadian nationalism and contemporary Acadian identity began around the 1860s. Over the next few decades, leaders who attended the Acadian National Conventions in the 1880s established national symbols and an Acadian holiday, August 15th, the feast day of the Assumption of the Virgin Mary (a recognition of Louis XIII's dedication of France to the Virgin Mary in the 17th Century, and thus an homage to the values of pre-Revolutionary France). The Acadian flag they adopted consisted of the French flag, with its vertical bands of blue, white, and red, to which a gold star was added in the upper left corner representing the Virgin Mary. The Acadian community also adopted a national hymn, "Ave Maris Stella," which is traditionally sung in both Latin and French.

Today, Acadians have overcome many challenges to create a vibrant francophone cultural presence in Atlantic Canada and beyond. They are present in business, politics, the arts, and other areas of civic life. They have founded French-language educational institutions, such as Collège St. Joseph (established in 1864) in New Brunswick, Université Sainte-Anne (founded in 1890) in Nova Scotia, and Université de Moncton (founded in 1963), and Acadian children receive French first-language education. Acadian festivals throughout the Maritime Provinces showcase Acadian arts, culture, and music.

Since 1994, Acadians from around the world have gathered every five years for the Congrès Mondial Acadien (World Acadian Congress), which seeks to bring together the various parts of the Acadian diaspora. Over the 10-day congress, visitors can take in Acadian music and culture, sample Acadian food, and participate in family reunions.

The story of the Acadians is an incredible saga of perseverance and devotion to a culture and way of life. Moyse de les Dernier, a Swiss Protestant serving the British Governor of Nova Scotia, visited the settlements of the Acadian heartlands in the 1770s and provided one of the few written accounts of Acadia prior to the Deportation. He described the Acadians as the "most innocent and virtuous people" he had known and praised their hospitality and *joie de vivre*. He characterized the Acadians' simple lives living off the land, free from class distinctions, as a sort of Golden Age.

ACADIAN FRENCH Acadian French has some unique features that make it distinct from both the French spoken in France, and from the French in other French-speaking parts of Canada. The relative isolation of the Acadians from the rest of the French-speaking world for almost three centuries led to the preservation of aspects of 17th-century French that were lost elsewhere, as well as the continued use of several old words from the centre-west area of France, south of the Loire River, from which most Acadians had emigrated. A few of these unusual features include:

- Use of the first person plural *je* rather than *nous* (we), as in *je mangeons* (we eat) or *j'avions eu* (we had)
- Use of *à* to situate events in time, for example *à soir* (tonight) or *à matin* (this morning)
- Words common in the area just south of the Loire River in France, such as *charrette* (cart) and *barge* (haystack)
- Use of the simple past tense such as *ils coupirent* (they cut) or *je fus* (I was), which has completely disappeared from spoken French in other parts of the world
- The use of the word *point* to denote negation instead of *ne . . . pas*, as in *j'ai point de pommes* (I don't have any apples)
- Words such as *bailler* (to give), *mitan* (middle), *noirceur* (darkness), and *menterie* (lie) from Old French

The French spoken by Acadians is in many ways reminiscent of the language found in the 17th-century writings of Molière, France's most celebrated playwright. Thanks to their familiarity with vocabulary, syntax, and pronunciations that mirror those of 17th-century French, Acadians have performed many of Molière's plays in France and around the world. Acadian French also incorporates words derived from English and Indigenous languages, such as *boucane* (smoke).

Although some of the words and uses are in decline (perhaps due to exposure to a more standard French in schools, and greater contact with other French-speaking regions), many of the features that make Acadian French unique have persisted to this day.

THE ACADIAN TABLE

THE UNMISTAKABLE AROMA of meat pie baking in the oven, rich fragrant broth bubbling on the stovetop for the evening's *fricot*, buckwheat pancakes frying in a cast iron pan waiting to be topped with molasses—these are the sights and smells of a traditional Acadian kitchen. The rustic cuisine of the Acadians encompasses a wide range of dishes developed in home kitchens in Nova Scotia, New Brunswick, Prince Edward Island, Northern Maine, Louisiana, and beyond. Most Acadian recipes can be made from inexpensive pantry staples and local produce, with a bit of time and effort.

Like many Acadians, I have fond memories of family meals and get-togethers, which always revolved around food and where Acadian specialities took centre stage. From the magnificent spreads of meat pie and molasses-laced desserts served at the traditional Acadian *Réveillon* on Christmas Eve, to family gatherings where hearty *chaudrée* or *poutine râpée* were shared, many of these dishes are rooted in centuries-old traditions, along with some more recent creations.

FLAVOURS OF HOME Acadian food originated in the French culinary traditions of the 17th century, which were adapted to the new environments in which the Acadians lived. The result was a unique and creative cuisine that revolved around the seasons and way of life of the people who prepared it. Acadian cooking has always been by its very nature local and seasonal, making the most of the produce that could be grown and foraged locally. Using these readily available ingredients, Acadians produced some highly inventive dishes, sometimes born of necessity, sometimes of pure creativity. Much like Italy's *cucina povera*, many of these recipes were created by making use of everyday ingredients in novel and unusual ways, ensuring that nothing went to waste. Acadian food isn't about fussy techniques and preparations—it's about taking simple, local ingredients and turning them into a delicious meal. Indeed, one of the unifying characteristics of Acadian cooking is its simplicity. Many Acadian dishes, such as fricot and jambalaya, can be cooked in one pot, and Acadian meals traditionally revolve around a single hearty course. A number of classic Acadian dishes have remained largely unchanged for hundreds of years. Many dishes that featured on 18th- or 19th-century Acadian tables would be easily recognizable to those familiar with Acadian cooking today, and these are some of the dishes that we have included in this book to share with you.

The simple approach to food and cooking developed by Acadians turned out to be healthy as well, providing a wholesome, balanced diet. Traditional Acadian fare includes large amounts of fish, seafood, and locally grown vegetables, which provided the sustenance required for long days of work on fishing vessels or on the farm. This approach to cooking no doubt contributed to the fact that Acadians were known for living long lives, as well as for their vigour in old age.

A CUISINE SHAPED BY HISTORY, CLIMATE, AND CULTURAL EXCHANGE Acadian food is rooted in the traditions of 17th-century French cooking, specifically the dishes of the centre-west region of France where most Acadian colonists emigrated from. The origins of a number of Acadian dishes, such as chaudrée, can be traced back to this region.

The climate and landscape of the Acadians' new homeland had a discernible impact on the food they prepared. To make it through the long cold winters they faced, a variety of preserving methods were used to extend the shelf life of vegetables, fruits, meat, and fish. This accounts for the liberal use of pickled, smoked, dried, and salted ingredients and accompaniments in traditional Acadian cooking. The Acadians also foraged for wild fruits and plants they found in their new homeland, some of which would have been unfamiliar to the French colonists, and incorporated them into their cooking. Many of these wild plants, fruits, and herbs or their cultivated cousins can still be found in Acadian recipes today.

Although a great many dishes were preserved and passed on from generation to generation, Acadian cooking did not remain cut off from the rest of the world, and it was shaped in various ways through contact with other cultures. This influence occurred through the introduction of new foods, such as maple syrup, the production of which was passed on to the Acadians by Indigenous peoples to be used in sweets and desserts.

Similarly, the Cajuns adopted new ingredients such as rice, crawfish, and chilies into their recipes, and were influenced by the Spanish and Creole cultures they encountered in their new home in Louisiana. These exchanges resulted in new twists on traditional Acadian dishes such as *boudin*, and introduced new recipes to Acadian cuisine such as gumbo and jambalaya.

Historical events also played a role in shaping Acadian cooking in various ways, the most notable being the Deportation. While prior to the Deportation Acadians continued the agrarian traditions brought over from France, in the years following the Deportation those who resettled in the Maritime provinces lived to a much greater extent from the sea. Fish and shellfish became an important part of the Acadian diet from this period onwards. Acadians also made greater use of ingredients that grew more readily in the rocky soils of the areas where many settled after the Deportation, especially potatoes, of which they grew particularly fond.

RELIGIOUS CULINARY TRADITIONS The Acadians' eating habits were influenced by the traditions of the Catholic faith that they brought with them to the New World. Many religious holidays were celebrated with special foods and recipes, while certain foods were avoided during other times of the year, according to Catholic tradition.

On the night of the Epiphany on January 6th, a *galette des rois* or Twelfth Night cake was traditionally served in Acadie. Various trinkets were baked into the cake, such as a button, ring, medal, or dry bean, depending on the region. Once the cake was cut and portioned, it was said that the person who uncovered the ring would marry soon, the person who received the medal was destined for a religious vocation, and the person who found the bean was crowned king or queen and presided over the evening's festivities. The person who received the button would supposedly remain a bachelor or an old maid.

Acadians celebrated Candlemas on February 5th to coincide with the blessing of candles at church. According to the custom, Candlemas pancakes, or *crêpes de la Chandeleur*, were prepared and each person was responsible for flipping their

own pancake. Like the galette des rois, these pancakes sometimes contained small trinkets to which particular meanings were ascribed.

The days leading up to Lent were known as the *jours gras*, or fat days, by the Acadians, culminating in the *Mardi Gras* (Shrove Tuesday) celebrations. It was a time of feasting, drinking, and entertainment before the 40 days of penitence that would follow. On Mardi Gras, Acadians confected a type of pulled-sugar maple candy known as *tire*, which was also sometimes made from molasses. All of the tire had to be consumed before midnight and the beginning of Lent.

During Lent, Acadians observed a period of fasting and penitence, as prescribed by the church. Meat was prohibited on certain days and sweets and other rich foods were generally avoided. During this period, Acadians ate fish on days that they could not eat meat.

On Easter Sunday, the tradition in Acadian households was to serve eggs cooked in various ways throughout the day. Eggs were often saved up for weeks in anticipation, at which point they would be served boiled, in omelettes, and in the form of a flan with maple syrup or maple sugar.

For the *Toussaint* (or All Saints' Day) on November 1st, Acadians prepared a cabbage soup with salt pork and *herbes salées* known as *soupe de la Toussaint*, or All Saints' Day soup. The day was also known as the *jour des tours*, or "day of tricks," as the custom was to steal a cabbage from your neighbour's garden on All Saints' Eve for the soup.

Acadian Christmas celebrations centred on midnight mass. Like French-speaking peoples in other parts of the world, many Acadians partake in the custom of Réveillon, a sumptuous repast taken after midnight mass. A traditional Acadian Réveillon might include a meat pie (see page 116), *râpure* (see page 72), or *poutine râpée* (see page 69) depending on the region, as well as several types of sweets. On Christmas day, roast goose was the most favoured choice of bird to grace the Acadian table. Special homemade cookies called *naulets* were given to children at Christmas time. Sweetened with sugar or molasses, they were cut in the shape of a small child to symbolize the baby Jesus.

STAR INGREDIENTS Though most Acadian dishes are made from everyday ingredients, there are a handful of ingredients that come up again and again in Acadian cooking, imparting a distinctively Acadian flavour to the dishes in which they are used:

HERBES SALÉES or salted herbs are an indispensable ingredient in classic Acadian cooking. Traditionally made from a combination of chives, shallots, onion shoots, and wild herbs, they are used as a seasoning in a wide range of dishes, from soups to fish courses.

WARMING SPICES such as cloves, cinnamon, nutmeg, and pepper feature heavily in traditional Acadian cuisine. The liberal use of exotic spices in both sweet and savoury dishes, a vestige of medieval European cookery that fell out of favour in France in the late 17th and 18th centuries, was preserved in the Acadian culinary tradition.

MOLASSES or *mélasse*, as it is known by the Acadians, is an important ingredient in Acadian cooking. It is used in baking and as a topping for *ployes*, a traditional Acadian pancake, and râpure (or rappie pie), a savoury potato-and-meat dish popular in southwestern Nova Scotia and Prince Edward Island. In many Acadian households, a slice of bread topped with molasses was served in lieu of dessert, a tradition known as *pain à la mélasse*.

POTATOES, although they were not a major part of the Acadian diet prior to the Deportation, would become a staple of Acadian cooking in the decades after 1755. Potatoes are now used to prepare many classic Acadian dishes, including fricot, rappie pie, poutine râpée, and chaudrée.

SALTED AND SMOKED FISH were traditionally both consumed by the Acadians, and turn up in many dishes. At one time, most Acadian families had a smoke-house where they could prepare smoked fish (which they called *poisson boucané*) by laying salted fish over a small sawdust fire that was kept burning. Acadians were particularly fond of smoked herring, which was served cold or warm with bread and butter. See the method for salting fish on page 85.

PORK was the favourite meat of the Acadians according to historical accounts. It was consumed fresh, particularly in the winter and around Christmas, as was salted pork. Pork is used in the traditional Acadian *pâté à la viande*—or meat pie—and to make boudin, an Acadian blood pudding.

CHILIES, HOT SAUCE, AND CAYENNE PEPPER are used by cooks in Louisiana to inject a bit of heat and Southern flavour into various dishes, such as Cajun jambalaya.

SUMMER SAVORY, which grows particularly well in the Atlantic Canadian climate, adds fragrant herbal notes to many Acadian dishes.

CLASSIC ACADIAN RECIPES The Acadian culinary repertoire contains a number of classic dishes that are common across Acadian regions. Many of these recipes are based on simple cooking techniques that were easily adapted to make use of different ingredients, and to appeal to local tastes:

FRICOT is the one quintessentially Acadian dish. This hearty soup made from broth, summer savory, potatoes, and meat, fish, or seafood, is popular throughout Acadie. In southwestern Nova Scotia chicken is typically used, though other variations include rabbit or beef. In northwestern New Brunswick, fricot is often made with fish or seafood, mackerel being one of the most common choices. It can also be made with trout, cod, eel, and even clams, known as *fricot aux coques*. In some regions fricot also includes dumplings called *poutines*.

CHAUDRÉE is a fish soup that is another staple of the Acadian diet, named after the pot it was cooked in, a *chaudron*. An Acadian import from the Saintonge region of France, it originally included salt pork, though in most modern-day recipes this has been replaced with more fish and seafood. The soup is thickened first with flour, then potatoes, and eventually cream. Chaudrée was taken up in the English-speaking parts of North America, who anglicized its name to chowder.

BOUDIN is a traditional Acadian blood pudding made from pork meat and offal, pork blood, onions, and spices such as cloves and summer savory. At one time, every Acadian family made their own boudin, and it was eaten at various mealtimes, including breakfast. The Cajuns add rice, hot peppers, and cayenne pepper to make their decidedly spicier take on boudin.

PÂTÉ À LA VIANDE OR MEAT PIE is a dish that no traditional Acadian Christmas would be complete without. Classic meat pie was made from shredded pork meat mixed with spices, though today it is often combined with chicken, rabbit, or beef. Each Acadian region has its own variation on meat pie, with its distinct combination of meats and unique style of pastry, which is traditionally made with lard. The humble potato served as the base for two unique but remarkably similar Acadian dishes that were developed in different parts of Acadie. **RÂPURE OR RAPPIE PIE** is a dish made from potatoes and meat that is popular in Nova Scotia and Prince Edward Island. The base is made from grated potatoes from which the water has been extracted, and chicken, pork, rabbit, or even seafood is added. The result is a flavoursome mixture with a somewhat gelatinous texture that is baked in the oven. Cubes of pork fat placed on top of the rappie pie help give it its characteristic crispy crust, which is particularly prized. **POUTINES RÂPÉES**, found in southeastern New Brunswick, are potato dumplings with a gluey texture that are extremely popular. In some areas they are made with pork in the centre, while in others they are prepared without meat.

JAMBALAYA is a rice and sausage dish from Lousiana's Cajun district, and a perennial favourite. Most likely derived from Spanish paella, the Cajuns put their own unique spin on this classic Louisiana dish. Cajun jambalaya is typically made by browning pork sausage to which onions, bell peppers, various herbs, spices, chicken broth, and rice are added. Some variations also include ham, chicken, or crustaceans, such as shrimp or crawfish.

PLOYES, a type of buckwheat pancake, are an Acadian speciality from northwestern New Brunswick. Made from a combination of wheat and buckwheat flour, they are traditionally served as an accompaniment to savoury dishes. They can also be topped with molasses, sugar, or maple syrup to provide a sweet end to a meal.

Acadians have always been fond of sweets which were served, sometimes even as an accompaniment to the main course, to mark special occasions and honoured guests. **GALETTES À LA MÉLASSE** or **MOLASSES COOKIES** (see recipe page 205) were one of the most popular sweets made by the Acadians. Flavoured with spices such as ginger, cinnamon, and cloves, molasses gives the cookies their dark brown colour. Acadians also made several types of French-style doughnuts known as **BEIGNES** or **BEIGNETS**. These were traditionally served at weddings, banquets, and at Christmas. Among the different types of beignets are ones made with buttermilk, molasses, potatoes, and a yeasted version popular among the Cajuns in Louisiana.

INTRODUCTION TO THE RECIPES

ACADIAN FOOD HAS always combined the best of tradition with new ideas and ingredients. It continues to evolve to this day, incorporating techniques and influences from cuisines from other parts of the world. With Acadian and Cajun chefs and home cooks experimenting with new ingredients and reinventing old classics, Acadian cuisine is certainly still alive and well today.

Over the next chapters, I want to share with you recipes that fit into this gamut of time and influences. The recipes are a mix of traditional and family sourced, along with some of my own creations. My knowledge of Acadian food started at home and in my grandmother's kitchen in Edmundston, New Brunswick, and I now pass these experiences on to you.

SALADS AND APPETIZERS

OYSTERS RAW WITH TWO MIGNONETTES
Huîtres Natures avec Deux Mignonettes

AS OYSTERS WERE such a staple in the Acadian diet, I thought we would share how to shuck fresh oysters step by step and accompany it with some popular mignonettes that the new generation of raw oyster eaters are all talking about. Oysters have come a long way my friends, but the traditions are still alive and well.

HOW TO SHUCK AN OYSTER

Shucking an oyster ideally requires an oyster knife with a short, sharp, thick blade. Wear a glove to protect your hand against the knife and sharp edges of the shell.

STEP 1 Hold your oyster with the deep side of the shell down and the hinge toward you. Secure the oyster on a towel against a hard surface.

STEP 2 Insert the knife between the shells near the hinge, twisting the knife to separate the halves.

STEP 3 The oyster is attached to the centre of its upper and lower shells by a strong muscle. With the knife, slide across the inside of the top shell to sever the muscle attached to the upper shell.

STEP 4 Lift off and discard the upper shell.

STEP 5 Slide the knife across the inside of the bottom shell and sever the lower muscle, removing any grit or shell. Take care not to spill the delicious salty liquor in the shell. Partially attached meat is messy to eat.

Your oyster is now ready to be eaten raw or prepared. I recommend serving with a mignonette (an accompaniment for oysters that enhances their flavour). Add 1 tsp (5 mL) to every oyster and sip away.

SPICY APPLE AND SHALLOT MIGNONETTE

In a large jar, add vinegar, wine, sugar, shallots, apple, and pepper sauce; cover and shake well. Let rest in refrigerator for at least 1 hour. Mignonette will keep for few weeks refrigerated.

 If honey crisp apple is not available you can substitute with any cruchy sweet apple.

MAKES 2 CUPS (500 ML)

½ cup (125 mL) cider vinegar
½ cup (125 mL) white wine
½ cup (125 mL) sugar
½ cup (125 mL) finely diced shallots
¼ cup (60 mL) diced honey crisp apple
1 Tbsp (15 mL) hot pepper sauce

HERB AND HONEY MIGNONETTE

In a large jar, add vinegar, wine, honey, shallots, and herbs; cover and shake well. Let rest in refrigerator for at least 1 hour. Mignonette will keep for a few weeks refrigerated.

MAKES 2 CUPS (500 ML)

½ cup (125 mL) rice wine vinegar
½ cup (125 mL) white wine
½ cup (125 mL) honey
½ cup (125 mL) finely diced shallots
¼ cup (60 mL) mixed herbs (such as parsley, tarragon, and chives)

OYSTERS FLYNN
Huîtres à la Flynn

MAKES 2 SERVINGS

1 dozen large oysters
1 sleeve saltine or soda
   crackers (about 25 crackers)
1 tsp (5 mL) salt
1 tsp (5 mL) freshly ground
   pepper
2 Tbsp (30 mL) butter
Tartar sauce, for serving

MANY OF OUR Acadian ancestors lived by the sea, and the foods that they were able to harvest from the waters played a very important role in their diets. Oysters were no exception. This recipe pays tribute to the mother of a good friend of mine; Agnes Matilda Flynn was not only an excellent cook but an experimental one, and her son Johnny is a renowned oyster farmer in Prince Edward Island who grows Colville Bay oysters. This recipe is one that I have fallen in love with. Don't be fooled by the simplicity of it—Mrs. Flynn's oysters have an amazing flavour.

Shuck oysters (see page 22 on how to shuck) and set meats aside. Place crackers in a Ziploc bag and use a rolling pin to make a very fine crumb. Place crumbs on a plate and add in the salt and freshly ground pepper. Roll oyster meats in the crumbs.

In a large frying pan, melt butter and fry oysters on each side until golden brown, about 1 minute per side. Serve as is or with a side of your favourite tartar sauce.

SIMPLE STEAMED MUSSELS
Moules à la Vapeur Simples

ACADIANS HAVE ALWAYS had a great love of seafood and wild mussels in particular. Mussels are extremely versatile—they are like little sponges, taking on the characteristics of the flavours they encounter. Having said that, I still enjoy this classic way of preparing mussels above all others. Sometimes simple is best and a little can go a long way.

Place mussels in a medium pot. Add in white wine, green onions, garlic, and lemon juice. Cover and steam over high heat for 5 to 6 minutes, until steam barrels out from under the lid. Avoid overcooking as this will cause the meat inside the mussels to shrink.

Serve mussels with melted butter for dipping. Any leftover broth can be frozen and used in chowders or other recipes.

MAKES 2 SERVINGS

2 lb (900 g) mussels
½ cup (125 mL) white wine
2 green onions, chopped
2 cloves garlic, finely chopped
1 Tbsp (15 mL) lemon juice
Melted butter, for serving

MOM'S SLAW
La Salade de Chou de Maman

MAKES 4 CUPS (1 L)

DRESSING

1 cup (250 mL) sugar
¾ cup (175 mL) white vinegar
¾ cup (175 mL) vegetable oil
1½ cups (375 mL) tomato
   soup
2 garlic cloves, cut in quarters
1 Tbsp (15 mL) HP sauce
1 tsp (5 mL) salt
1 tsp (5 mL) freshly ground
   pepper
1 tsp (5 mL) dry mustard

SLAW

1 head of white cabbage,
   shredded
½ head of red cabbage,
   shredded
2 carrots, peeled and grated

MY MOM'S COLESLAW is like no other. We have all come to expect a creamy coleslaw or vinegar based coleslaw, but this one has a tomato base and it makes for a refreshing change. I have used this in many restaurants over the years to enhance pulled pork, as an accompaniment to roasted chicken, and on many buffets. At our house, serving this slaw was a Christmas tradition that the entire family looked forward to and enjoyed.

In a large Mason jar, add sugar, vinegar, vegetable oil, tomato soup, garlic, HP sauce, salt, freshly ground pepper, and mustard. Mix together and refrigerate for 1 hour.

In a large bowl, combine white and red cabbage and toss together with carrots. Mix the slaw with the dressing as needed or serve the dressing on the side.

SPRING LETTUCE SALAD
Salade Printanière

ACADIANS WERE WELL known for having large gardens; they preserved, canned, bottled, and in later years froze the harvest to have during the long winter months. They were thankful to have that bounty, but I think everyone was relieved when spring came and fresh produce was once again available. We always looked forward to a salad that my Mom made with the first new lettuce leaves of the season. She made a unique dressing just for her spring lettuce salad using milk—it was one of my Dad's favourites.

Wash and dry all the vegetables and place in a large bowl. Add dressing to vegetables and serve.

MAKES 4 SERVINGS

24 lettuce leaves (you can substitute half with dandelion leaves)
6 radishes, cut into quarters
4 green onions (spring onions), chopped
Pinch of salt
¼ tsp (1 mL) freshly ground pepper
½ cup (125 mL) Spring Dressing (recipe follows)

SPRING DRESSING

In a large Mason jar, add mayonnaise, white vinegar, sugar, milk, salt, and freshly ground pepper; cover and shake vigorously. Refrigerate for up to 1 week.

MAKES ½ CUP (125 ML)

1 Tbsp (15 mL) mayonnaise
¼ cup (60 mL) white vinegar
1 tsp (5 mL) sugar
¼ cup (60 mL) whole milk
Salt to taste
Freshly ground pepper to taste

CHEF SALAD
La Salade du Chef

MAKES 2 SERVINGS

1 head iceberg lettuce, cored
   and roughly chopped
4 oz (115 g) cooked ham,
   julienned
4 oz (115 g) cooked turkey
   breast, sliced
8 slices of tomato
8 slices of cucumber
½ cup (125 mL) shredded old
   white cheddar
2 eggs, hard boiled and sliced
1 carrot, peeled and shredded
¼ cup (60 mL) Maple
   Vinaigrette (recipe follows)

AN OLD CLASSIC! A chef salad is a favourite from my early years of cooking in restaurants. It was the restaurant version of a cold plate without the potatoes. It was also the salad served at every church supper I attended in my youth. We've jazzed it up with a beautiful maple vinaigrette, which is a nice change from the French or Italian dressings that were served with it back in the day.

To assemble, split all ingredients between 2 bowls. For the classic presentation start with a bed of iceberg lettuce, then place ham and turkey next to each other in a row running down the centre of the bowl, and place tomato slices beside ham and cucumber slices beside the turkey. Place cheese alongside the tomato and sliced egg beside the cucumber. Top with grated carrot. Drizzle vinaigrette on the salad.

MAPLE VINAIGRETTE

MAKES 1¼ CUPS (310 ML)

1 clove of garlic, crushed
Pinch of salt
Pinch of freshly ground pepper
1 tsp (5 mL) Dijon mustard
¼ cup (60 mL) maple syrup
¼ cup (60 mL) balsamic
   vinegar
¾ cup (175 mL) vegetable oil

In a Mason jar, add garlic, salt, freshly ground pepper, Dijon mustard, maple syrup, balsamic vinegar, and vegetable oil and shake vigorously. Refrigerate for up to 2 weeks.

 Feel free to rearrange salad ingredients according to your preference.

PIGS IN A BLANKET
Saucisses en Croûte

PIGS IN A BLANKET are a real 60s snack. Watching Hockey Night in Canada when I was growing up, I couldn't wait for the first period intermission because we would have pigs in a blanket. Mom made them with Pillsbury pastry (the kind that came in a cardboard tube) and leftover hot dogs, and boy did we love them! Believe it or not they are making a comeback as gourmet sausages and pastry served with high end mustards. Everything old is new again.

Preheat oven to 375°F (190°C).

Roll out pie dough to a ¼-inch (0.5 cm) thick and cut into 1-inch (2.5 cm) strips. Cut lengthwise long enough to wrap around a sausage piece. Place a piece of sausage on each strip and roll it up. Roll between your hands to seal pastry and place on a cookie sheet. In a small bowl, mix egg and water together and brush on the outside of the pastry. Bake for 25 minutes or until pastry is golden brown. Dip Pigs in a Blanket into mustard sauce and enjoy.

MAKES 12 PASTRIES

1 savoury Pie Dough (see page 186)
4 chorizo sausages, baked and cut into thirds
1 egg, beaten
1 Tbsp (15 mL) water
Sweet and Savoury Mustard Sauce, for serving (recipe follows)

SWEET AND SAVOURY MUSTARD SAUCE

In a small bowl, mix all ingredients together and let sit for 10 minutes.

MAKES ¾ CUP (175 ML)

½ cup (125 mL) prepared yellow mustard
1 Tbsp (15 mL) HP sauce
2 Tbsp (30 mL) honey
2 Tbsp (30 mL) finely diced shallots
2 chives, chopped

MEDITERRANEAN-STYLE BAKED OYSTERS
Huîtres Méditerranéennes

MAKES 4 SERVINGS

1 medium tomato, diced
¼ cup (60 mL) diced black
   olives
1 medium shallot, diced
6 sprigs of fresh cilantro,
   chopped + extra for garnish
2 Tbsp (30 mL) olive oil
½ lime, juiced
½ tsp (2 mL) coarse sea salt
½ tsp (2 mL) freshly ground
   black pepper
16 large oysters, shucked on
   the half shell
¼ cup (60 mL) feta cheese

OYSTERS HAVE BEEN gathered on the shore and eaten straight from the shell for centuries. It wasn't until later that eating oysters became a social thing, usually with a few simple condiments such as pepper or citrus. Today, oysters have become hugely popular and the condiments have advanced as well: hot sauces and mignonettes are especially popular. For those who aren't fans of slurping, there are baked recipes like the one below.

Preheat oven to 350°F (175°C).

In a small bowl, mix tomato, olives, and shallot, then incorporate cilantro, olive oil, lime juice, sea salt, and freshly ground pepper; mix well.

Place oysters on a cookie sheet and bake for 4 to 5 minutes. Remove from oven; using a tablespoon, fill each oyster shell with stuffing and top with feta cheese. Set oven to broil and bake for another 3 to 4 minutes. Garnish with cilantro.

MEAT SPREAD
Creton à la Viande

CRETON IS A traditional meat spread that it quite often served on toast. Personally, I like mine on well-toasted crusty bread topped with old-fashioned yellow mustard. It can also be served as a lovely country pâté with a side of crackers. My favourite creton recipe comes from Chef Don Thibault, Chef Instructor at l'Ecole d'Hotellerie Edmundston, my Alma Mater. It's easy to make, full of flavours, and, best of all, it's not too fatty.

Preheat oven to 350°F (175°C).

In a heavy roasting pan, place pork shoulder and pork fat. Put into pre-heated oven for 1 hour. Remove from oven and add onion, celery, and garlic to the pan, then cook for another 30 minutes.

When cooking time has completed, run everything through a meat grinder twice, spread the mixture back on the roasting pan and place the pan on the stove on a medium-low heat. Add chicken broth, salt, freshly ground pepper, cinnamon, and cloves. Let simmer on low for 10 minutes. Pour into molds and let cool. Refrigerate overnight before unmoulding.

Creton freezes very well and can be kept in the freezer for up to 1 year.

FILLS SIX 4- × 9-INCH
(10 × 23 CM) MOLDS

5 lb (2.25 kg) pork shoulder, cut into 2-inch (5 cm) cubes
2 lb (900 g) pork fat, cut into 2-inch (5 cm) cubes
1 medium onion, diced
1 cup (250 mL) chopped celery
2 cloves garlic, minced
2 cups (500 mL) chicken broth
2 Tbsp (30 mL) salt
1 tsp (5 mL) freshly ground pepper
½ tsp (2 mL) cinnamon
¼ tsp (1 mL) ground cloves

DEVILED EGGS
Ouefs Farcis

MAKES 12 DEVILED EGGS

6 eggs, hard boiled and peeled
3 Tbsp (45 mL) mayonnaise
¼ tsp (1 mL) salt
½ tsp (2 mL) freshly ground
   pepper
½ tsp (2 mL) curry powder
1 Tbsp (15 mL) chopped
   chives, divided

WHEN IT CAME to social gatherings, pot lucks, and family get-togethers, the deviled egg was king back in the 60s and 70s. This recipe was very easy to prepare and it looked great on the table. Often, because it was so simple, making it was delegated to one of the older kids. The key to the recipe's success is in knowing how to cook the perfect egg.

Cut eggs in half lengthwise and place yolks in a small bowl; use a fork to mash the yolks. Add mayonnaise and mix well. Add salt, freshly ground pepper, curry powder, and half of the chives; mix well. Place filling into a plastic bag and snip the corner. Arrange whites on a platter and pipe filling into the centres. Garnish with remaining chives.

PERFECTLY BOILED EGGS

On the bottom of a heavy bottomed saucepan, place eggs in a single layer. Cover to the top of the eggs with cold water. Place eggs over medium-high heat and bring to a boil. As soon as the water reaches its boiling point, cover the pot and remove from heat. Allow eggs to stand for 12 to 14 minutes, uncover, and run a steady stream of cold water over the eggs for 2 to 3 minutes. Remove shells while eggs are still warm. The older the eggs are, the easier they are to peel.

BAR CLAM CEVICHE
Ceviche aux Palourdes

MAKES 4 SERVINGS

1 cup (250 mL) bar clam meat
¼ red onion, finely diced
4 sprigs of cilantro, chopped, divided
1 small chili pepper, sliced
½ tsp (2 mL) sea salt
¼ tsp (1 mL) freshly ground pepper
4 limes, juiced
1 Tbsp (15 mL) olive oil

BAR CLAMS ARE very meaty and that makes them a favourite of many people. Dug at low tide on sand bars, those that know how best to find them will say to go looking during a full moon. Many people cook bar clams and bottle them for winter; they are delicious enjoyed right out of the jar.

A few years back I had the pleasure of being a part of the "Clammin n' Jammin Festival" in Abrams Village, Prince Edward Island, where I entered into a contest for the best quahog or bar clam dish. Because I was going up against local quahog and bar clam aficionados I was less than confident about my chances, but luck was on my side—I made this bar clam ceviche and actually won.

Place bar clam meat on a cutting board and coarsely chop. Place in a small bowl and add in red onion and half of the cilantro. Add chili pepper, sea salt, and freshly ground pepper, and mix well; refrigerate until time to serve.

Just prior to serving, add lime juice and olive oil and gently toss. To serve, garnish with remaining cilantro.

PICKLED HERRING
Hareng Mariné

FOR ACADIANS LIVING on the shoreline, herring fishing was a part of life and pickling, salting, and smoking were common ways to preserve the fish for the year. This fun-to-make recipe focuses on pickling. It's simple to do and very tasty—I love to eat mine with a bit of sour cream, crusty bread, and a glass of bubbly (or a cold beer).

Rinse herring under cold water. Keep water running and hold fish under the water; descale by running a sharp knife from tail to head. Once descaled, slice the belly and remove the innards, then rinse the cavity. Fillet both sides of the fish and discard the carcass. Trim the belly side and remove the top fin. Cut diagonally into 1-inch (2.5 cm) pieces; each fillet should yield 3 to 4 pieces. Place fish pieces in a colander and rinse thoroughly. Place fish in a container with a lid, sprinkle with salt, and cover with cold water. Refrigerate for 24 hours.

The following day prepare the pickling liquid. In a medium saucepan, combine vinegar, garlic, onion, sugar, freshly ground pepper, bay leaves, and pickling spice; bring to a boil, then reduce and simmer for 5 to 10 minutes or until onions soften. Cool.

Place fish in a colander and rinse well. Layer into a Mason jar, alternating fish and the onions from the pickling liquid. Place 1 bay leaf in each jar, pour cooled liquid over the fish and onion mixture, seal, and refrigerate for a minimum of 24 hours. Use within 2 to 3 months.

FILLS TWO 12-OZ (355 ML) JARS

6 to 8 herring
3 Tbsp (45 mL) sea salt
1½ cups (375 mL) white vinegar
1 clove garlic, sliced
1 medium onion, thinly sliced
3 Tbsp (45 mL) sugar
1 tsp (5 mL) freshly ground black pepper
2 bay leaves
2 tsp (10 mL) pickling spice

CHOWDERS, SOUPS, AND FRICOT

ACADIAN FISH CHOWDER
Chaudrée Acadienne au Poisson

MAKES 4 SERVINGS

3 Tbsp (45 mL) butter, divided
1 cup (250 mL) diced onion
2 cups (500 mL) diced peeled
  potatoes
1 Tbsp (15 mL) herbes salées
  (see page 173)
1 tsp (5 mL) salt
½ tsp (2 mL) freshly ground
  pepper
4 cups (1 L) milk (2 %)
2 cups (500 mL) water
½ lb (250 g) haddock, cubed
  into 2-inch (5 cm) pieces
½ lb (250 g) salmon, cubed
  into 2-inch (5 cm) pieces
½ cup (125 mL) evaporated
  milk

THE ACADIAN NAME for this recipe would be chaudrée, but translated into English it is chowder. For economic reasons, milk-based chowders in the mid 20th century were for everyday dining and cream-based chowders were commonly reserved for special occasions. The fish was usually basic and featured whatever was inexpensive and readily available; lobster, for example, would never make its way into Wednesday-night milk chowder. There were lots of potatoes for filler, and this chowder was often served with soda crackers, which were usually broken up and added to the chowder after serving to give it even more substance.

Melt 2 Tbsp (30 mL) butter in a large heavy bottomed pot; add onion and sauté until translucent, about 2 to 3 minutes. Add potatoes, herbes salées, salt, freshly ground pepper, milk, and water. Stir and bring to a boil, then simmer for 15 minutes, or until potatoes are fork tender. Add haddock and salmon and simmer for another 10 minutes. Add evaporated milk and simmer for 4 to 5 minutes. Add remaining 1 Tbsp (15 mL) butter just before serving.

SEAFOOD CHOWDER
Chaudrée aux Fruits du Mer

SEAFOOD CHOWDER MADE with cream was an absolute delicacy when it was available (and the cows were milking), served only on the most special of occasions, whereas everyday chowder tended to have less seafood and was made with milk. I particularly like this chowder because it's not thickened with flour as potatoes are used instead. Finishing it with Brie just puts it over the top!

Rinse mussels under fresh running water. Throw away any that do not close. Cover the bottom of a large pot with water and add mussels. Cover with a lid and cook on high for about 5 to 6 minutes, or until steam is pouring out from under the lid. Remove mussels from the broth, shuck meats from the shells, and reserve 4 cups (1 L) mussel broth. Set aside.

In a large pot, cook half of the potatoes and half of the shallots in water until tender; drain and puree. Set aside.

In a large pot, sauté bacon and remaining shallots. Add butter, corn, and celery until transparent; add Dijon mustard and deglaze the pot with white wine. Allow wine to reduce, then add the remainder of the diced potatoes, basil, bay leaves, and mussel broth. Bring to a boil then reduce heat to a gentle simmer until potatoes are just fork tender.

When potatoes are cooked, add mussel meat, coldwater shrimp, lobster meat, snow crab meat, seared scallops, brie, and pureed potato; cook for a further 5 minutes. Season with salt and freshly ground pepper; stir in cream and allow to heat through. Adjust seasoning to taste.

MAKES 6 TO 8 SERVINGS

5 lb (2.25 kg) mussels
2 lb (900 g) yellow-flesh potatoes (skin on), diced into 1-inch (2.5 cm) pieces, divided
2 shallots, diced, divided
4 oz (115 g) uncooked double-smoked bacon, diced into 1-inch (2.5 cm) pieces
2 Tbsp (30 mL) butter
6 ears of corn, kernels removed
½ cup (125 mL) diced celery
1 Tbsp (15 mL) Dijon mustard
½ cup (125 mL) dry white wine
3 Tbsp (45 mL) chopped fresh basil
2 bay leaves
4 cups (1 L) mussel broth
1 lb (450 g) coldwater shrimp
1 lb (450 g) lobster meat
1 lb (450 g) snow crab meat
1 lb (450 g) scallops, seared
1 small wheel of double cream brie, rind removed, sliced
Salt to taste
Freshly ground pepper to taste
2 cups (500 mL) cream (35%)

OYSTER CHOWDER
Chaudrée aux Huîtres

MAKES 2 TO 4 SERVINGS

36 raw oysters
4 cups (1 L) heavy cream
    (35%)
1 Tbsp (15 mL) butter
½ cup (125 mL) finely
    chopped celery
½ cup (125 mL) finely
    chopped onion
½ cup (125 mL) diced peeled
    potato, cooked
Pinch of salt + extra to taste
1 tsp (5 mL) celery seed
1½ tsp (7 mL) hot pepper
    sauce
1 Tbsp (15 mL) fresh lemon
    juice
1 Tbsp (15 mL) chopped
    parsley
1 Tbsp (15 mL) chopped chives
Freshly ground pepper to taste

ANYTHING THAT COULD be harvested rather than bought was sure to be an Acadian staple, as the winters were long and money was often scarce. In early Acadian times this chowder would have been made with cream from cows if available, but these days evaporated milk is used.

Shuck the oysters and separate the liquid and meats into separate containers; reserve the liquid. In a large heavy saucepan over medium heat, bring heavy cream and the oyster liquid to a simmer. Remove from heat and set aside.

Melt butter in a large sauté pan over medium heat. Add celery, onion, potato, and salt, and sweat for 2 to 3 minutes until onion is translucent. Add celery seed, hot pepper sauce, lemon juice, and oyster meats; cook for 1 to 2 minutes, or until the edges of the oysters start to curl.

Add the cream and oyster juice to meat the mixture and add parsley and chives. Season with salt and pepper and let simmer for 5 minutes, or until heated through.

DELICIOUS CORN CHOWDER
Délicieuse Chaudrée au Maïs

THIS IS A CORN chowder to warm your heart. In the winter, my Mom would include corn chowder on Thursdays in the weekly soup rotation, since we would have run out of meat by that point in the week. This recipe is easy to prepare and the use of canned corn makes it both economical and handy.

Place potatoes in a large pot and cover with salted water; boil until fork tender. Drain and divide into 2 halves, mashing one of the halves; set both mashed and remaining cubed potatoes aside.

In a sauté pan, fry bacon until crisp then set aside. Fry onion in the remaining bacon fat.

In a large pot, place onion and all-purpose flour, then cook over medium heat until flour has dissolved, stirring to ensure no lumps form. Add milk and stock, bring to a boil, and stir in salt, freshly ground pepper, bacon, creamed corn, corn nibblets, and the mashed and cubed potatoes. Gently heat until warmed through.

MAKES 4 TO 6 SERVINGS

2 lb (900 g) potatoes, peeled and cubed
1 lb (450 g) uncooked bacon, diced
1 large onion, chopped
¼ cup (60 mL) all-purpose flour
3 cups (750 mL) whole milk
3 cups (750 mL) chicken stock
½ tsp (2 mL) salt
½ tsp (2 mL) freshly ground pepper
Two 14-oz (400 g) cans creamed corn
Two 12-oz (355 g) cans corn nibblets

FIDDLEHEAD, APPLE, AND BEER SOUP

Potage à la Fougère, aux Pommes et à la Bière

MAKES 4 TO 6 SERVINGS

2 Tbsp (30 mL) butter
1 large onion, diced
½ cup (125 mL) celery, diced
1 lb (450 g) yellow-flesh pota-
    toes, peeled and diced
3 apples, chopped into 1-inch
    (2 cm) pieces
1 Tbsp (15 mL) Dijon mustard
1½ cups (375 mL) lager or
    beer of your choice
2 bay leaves
¼ tsp (1 mL) thyme
8 cups (2 L) frozen fiddle-
    heads, boiled until tender
6 cups (1.5 L) vegetable broth
½ cup (125 mL) maple syrup
2 cups (500 mL) cream (35%)
Salt to taste
Freshly ground pepper to taste
Sour cream, for garnish
    (optional)
Parmesan cheese, grated, for
    garnish (optional)

SOME OF MY fondest memories of growing up in northern New Brunswick centre on my years in the Boy Scouts. As part of an annual fundraiser, our troop would pile into cars at the break of dawn and spend hours scouring river banks searching for that springtime treasure—fiddle-heads. While we were gone, our parents were at home lining up buyers for our bounty. We were never left with unsold product! This soup takes me right back to those days.

Melt butter in a large saucepan and sauté onion and celery until translucent. Add potatoes, apple, and Dijon mustard; deglaze pan with beer. Add bay leaves, thyme, fiddleheads, and broth; bring to a boil, reduce heat, and simmer for 1 hour. Remove bay leaves and puree soup in a blender until smooth. Ladle into individual bowls and finish with maple syrup, cream, salt, and freshly ground pepper. Garnish with a dollop of sour cream and Parmesan cheese, if desired.

TOMATO HERBES SALÉES SOUP
Soupe aux Tomates et aux Herbes Salées

HERBES SALÉES WAS a staple in every Acadian kitchen. It was used for just about everything you needed to add flavour to, especially soup. There was always an abundance of tomatoes in the garden and this soup was a great way to use them up. Perfect accompanied by a grilled cheese sandwich, it's a classic combination that never grows old!

Score the bottom of each tomato with an X. In a large pot, cover fresh tomatoes with water, bring to a boil, and cook until skins begin to slip off. Remove tomatoes from water and remove skins; set aside.

In a heavy bottomed soup pot, sauté onions and garlic until soft. Add fresh tomatoes, crushed tomatoes, salt, freshly ground pepper, herbes salées, oregano, and chicken broth. Return to a boil and simmer for 15 minutes. Remove from heat and emulsify until smooth. Stir in parmesan cheese and cream. Return to heat and warm through. Garnish with your favourite herb.

MAKES 4 TO 6 SERVINGS

6 fresh tomatoes
1 cup (250 mL) diced onions
4 cloves garlic, minced
3½ cups (875 mL) canned
  crushed tomatoes
½ tsp (2 mL) salt
½ tsp (2 mL) freshly ground
  pepper
1 Tbsp (15 mL) herbes salées
  (see page 173)
½ tsp (2 mL) dry oregano
4 cups (1 L) chicken broth
1 cup (250 mL) parmesan
  cheese (powdered
  preferred)
½ cup (125 mL) cream (35%)
Herb of your choice, for
  garnish

FARMER'S WIFE SOUP
Soupe de la Fermière

LIFE WAS NOT easy for most Acadian families. Money wasn't always in abundance, so a vegetable soup was an economical way to feed a family, especially during harvest times. A fermière soup is a tribute to the hard-working wives of farmers.

Melt better in a large heavy bottomed soup pot and sauté onions, carrots, turnip, potatoes, and celery until they start to soften, about 7 to 8 minutes. Add Dijon mustard, herbes salées, summer savory, brown sugar, bay leaves, freshly ground pepper, and tomatoes. Add water and bring to a boil, then reduce heat and simmer for 1 hour. Add rice, barley, or small pasta during the last half hour of cooking.

 If summer savory is not available, sage can be substituted.

MAKES 4 TO 6 SERVINGS

2 Tbsp (30 mL) butter
1 cup (250 mL) chopped onions (1-inch/2.5-cm pieces)
1 cup (250 mL) sliced carrots
1 cup (250 mL) turnip, chopped into 1-inch (2.5cm) pieces
1 cup (250 mL) chopped peeled potatoes (1-inch/2.5-cm pieces)
½ cup (125 mL) celery, diced
1 Tbsp (15 mL) Dijon mustard
1 Tbsp (15 mL) herbes salées (see page 173)
1 tsp (5 mL) summer savory
1 tsp (5 mL) brown sugar
2 bay leaves
1 tsp (5 mL) freshly ground pepper
3½ cups (875 mL) canned diced tomatoes
8 cups (2 L) water
½ cup (125 mL) uncooked rice, barley, or small pasta

CABBAGE SOUP
Soupe aux Choux

MAKES 4 TO 6 SERVINGS

2 Tbsp (30 mL) butter

¾ cup (175 mL) diced onion

2 cups (500 mL) diced celery

4 medium carrots, peeled and diced

2 cloves garlic, minced

3½ cups (875 mL) fresh diced tomatoes

1 tsp (5 mL) dried marjoram

1 tsp (5 mL) dried parsley

1 tsp (5 mL) dried oregano

½ tsp (2 mL) dried thyme

1 tsp (5 mL) salt

1 tsp (5 mL) freshly ground pepper

8 cups (2 L) chicken broth

1 medium white cabbage, shredded into 1-inch (2.5 cm) pieces

4 medium potatoes, peeled and diced small

THE CABBAGE (LE CHOU) is a vegetable that stores very well over the winter and it was used by the whole community. At our house, we ate cabbage rolls, cabbage slaw, and of course cabbage soup. Because the cabbage itself is rather bland you really need spices to give it a punch. They say this soup is great for aiding in weight loss but although my family ate plenty, we did not experience this result!

In a large soup pot, add butter. Once melted, add onion, celery, carrots, and garlic; sauté until vegetables begin to soften, about 7 to 8 minutes. Add diced tomatoes, herbs, chicken broth, and shredded cabbage; bring to a boil. Reduce heat and simmer for 1½ hours, adding potatoes for the last half hour.

ACADIAN PEA SOUP
Soupe Ancestrale aux Pois

OLD-FASHIONED PEA soup, made the way your grand mama and her grand mama and her grand mama used to do it, is about taking the time to soak the dried peas and then simmer slowly for hours. In our home, it was served with fresh bread (see page 189). Today we make pea soup with split peas to save time and while it is still very good, nothing beats the old ways.

In a large bowl, add dried white peas, cover with water, soak for 3 hours, then simmer on medium-high heat for 10 minutes; strain and add to a Dutch oven. Add 1 gallon (4 L) water, salted pork, onion, and cloves. Bring to a boil and add salt and freshly ground pepper, then reduce heat and let simmer for 1 hour and 15 minutes. Add carrot and celery during the last 20 minutes of cooking. Remove cloves before serving.

MAKES 6 SERVINGS

1 cup (250 mL) dried white peas
1 gallon (4 L) water + extra for soaking peas
½ cup (125 mL) chopped salted pork
1 small onion
2 whole cloves
2 tsp (10 mL) salt
½ tsp (2 mL) freshly ground pepper
1 carrot, finely diced
½ cup (125 mL) finely diced celery

ACADIAN CHICKEN FRICOT
Fricot au Poulet Acadien

FRICOT WAS AND is a staple in many Acadian homes, and while different regions will vary in the preparation method, the method also varies from family to family within a region depending on which recipe has been handed down through the generations. It is widely recognized as a true Acadian dish!

In a large pot, boil chicken in 10 cups (2.5 L) water until tender, about 60 minutes. Remove chicken and strain and reserve the broth. Cool chicken and remove skin and meat from the bones. Roughly chop meat and set aside.

Return broth to the pot and add potatoes, onion, celery, carrots, bouillon, freshly ground pepper, summer savory, and chopped meat. Add water to cover if needed. Bring to a boil, reduce heat, and simmer for 45 minutes. Add dumplings during the final 20 minutes of cooking, if using. Spoon fricot into bowls and serve.

MAKES 4 TO 6 SERVINGS

One 5-lb (2.25 kg) whole chicken (bone in, skin on)
10 cups (2.5 L) water
8 medium potatoes, peeled and diced
1 medium onion, finely chopped
1 cup (250 mL) diced celery
3 carrots, peeled and diced
2 tsp (10 mL) chicken bouillon
1 tsp (5 mL) freshly ground pepper
1 tsp (5 mL) summer savory (or substitute with ½ tsp /2 mL thyme and ½ tsp /2 mL sage)
Fricot dumplings (optional; recipe follows)

FRICOT DUMPLINGS

In a large bowl, mix together flour, baking powder, and salt. Use a fork to gradually incorporate milk into the flour mixture. Using 2 teaspoons, drop dough into hot fricot or stew; cover pot and cook for 15 minutes, or until the dough is cooked through.

There are as many ways to form the dumplings as there are ways to make fricot—some folks like to roll them into small balls, some drop them into the hot liquid with a tablespoon or teaspoon. My mother liked to use a pair of scissors to cut the dough directly above the pot, allowing the dough to fall into the hot liquid. There is no right or wrong way.

MAKES 12 DUMPLINGS

1½ cups (375 mL) all-purpose flour
2¼ tsp (11 mL) baking powder
½ tsp (2 mL) salt
¾ cup (175 mL) whole milk

WILD RABBIT FRICOT
Fricot au Lapin des Bois

MAKES 4 SERVINGS

4 oz (115 g) uncooked country
   bacon, diced

3 Tbsp (45 mL) butter

One 3-lb (1.3 kg) wild rabbit
   (or 1 farmed rabbit),
   skinned, cleaned, and cut
   into 9 pieces

2 medium onions, diced

1 tsp (5 mL) salt

½ tsp (2 mL) freshly ground
   pepper

4 cups (1 L) diced peeled
   potatoes

2 cups (500 mL) chopped
   carrots (in thick chunks)

Fricot Dumplings (optional;
   see page 57)

SNARING RABBIT (LAPIN) was one of the best ways to eat from the land; it was also a great way to keep the young trappers busy. My two favourite ways to use small game, whether rabbit, partridge, or pheasant, is in a meat pie, Tourtière, or this amazing fricot.

In a deep cast iron pan, sauté country bacon until golden brown. Drain off fat and discard. Leave bacon in pan, add butter, and heat until melted. Add rabbit pieces, browning well on all sides. In a large, heavy bottomed pot, add bacon, rabbit, diced onion, salt, and freshly ground pepper. Add enough water to cover the meat by about 6 inches (15 cm). Bring to a boil, reduce heat, and simmer for 1½ hours. Add potatoes and carrots, cover, and cook for 10 minutes. Add dumplings, if desired, in teaspoon-sized drops and simmer until the dumplings have cooked.

 The same recipe can be used with partridge and small game.

CHICKEN FRICOT CHETICAMP
Fricot au Poulet, Style Cheticamp

WHILE IT IS not unusual to see many variations on fricot, this one is different from any other I have ever experienced. I discovered it while doing consulting work in a restaurant in Cheticamp, Nova Scotia. It's very hearty and easily serves as an entrée with no need for accompaniment. This is my version inspired by the ladies at the Old Cuisine et Artisanat Acadiens.

Dredge chicken thighs in all purpose-flour. In a large cast iron skillet, melt 2 Tbsp (30 mL) butter. Place chicken in the skillet and sear on both sides until golden, about 3 to 4 minutes; set aside.

In a large pot, melt the remaining 2 Tbsp (30 mL) butter and sauté onion and potatoes until onion becomes translucent. Add chicken thighs and pan juices and sprinkle with chives, salt, onion powder, and freshly ground pepper. Cover with water, bring to a boil, reduce to a simmer, and cook for 1 hour.

 You may add Fricot Dumplings to this recipe, if desired (see page 57).

MAKES 4 TO 6 SERVINGS

10 chicken thighs (bone in, skin on)
¼ cup (60 mL) all-purpose flour
¼ cup (60 mL) butter, divided
1 medium onion, finely chopped
4 cups (1 L) diced peeled potatoes
¼ cup (60 mL) dried chives
1½ tsp (7 mL) salt
1½ tsp (7 mL) onion powder
¼ tsp (1 mL) freshly ground pepper
10 cups (2.5 L) water

HAMBURGER VEGETABLE SOUP
Soupe de Viande Hachée et Légumes

MAKES 4 TO 6 SERVINGS

2 lb (900 g) ground beef
2 cups (500 mL) diced onions
2 cups (500 mL) diced carrots
2 cups (500 mL) diced peeled
    potatoes
1 cup (250 mL) diced celery
Two 14-oz (400 g) cans diced
    tomatoes with Italian herbs
2 bay leaves
2 Tbsp (30 mL) dried oregano
1 Tbsp (15 mL) dried basil
1 tsp (5 mL) salt
1 tsp (5 mL) freshly ground
    pepper
1 tsp (5 mL) dried thyme
1 tsp (5 mL) Louisiana hot
    sauce (or your favourite hot
    sauce)
6 cups (1.5 L) beef broth
½ cup (125 mL) barley

THIS CLASSIC HAMBURGER soup is a personal favourite. I've shared the recipe many times and without fail people will get back in touch to tell me how much they love it too. It was a staple growing up and the vegetables were always reflective of whatever was in season or in the fridge—it was never the same twice. It's perfect on a cold winter's night with bread or crackers.

In a large soup pot, fry ground beef until brown and add onions, carrots, potatoes, celery, and diced tomatoes; sauté until vegetables begin to soften, about 7 to 9 minutes. Add bay leaves, oregano, basil, salt, freshly ground pepper, thyme, hot sauce, beef broth, and barley. Bring to a boil, reduce heat, and simmer for 1 hour. Remove bay leaves before serving.

BEEF AND BARLEY SOUP
Soupe au Bœuf et à l'Orge

THIS IS A hearty and filling soup—the barley gives it a "stick to your ribs" quality. It's also a perfect "catch all," so feel free to throw in whatever you happen to have on hand. Leftover mushrooms, turnip, and broccoli have all made their way into this soup at one time or another.

In a large soup pot, heat butter and olive oil. Add stewing beef in small batches and brown, without overcrowding the pot, then set aside. Add more butter to the soup pot if necessary and sauté carrots, onions, and celery until soft. Add beef and all remaining ingredients. Bring to a boil, reduce to a simmer, and cook for 45 minutes.

Add a loaf of crusty bread and a glass of red wine and it's a perfect midweek dinner.

MAKES 4 TO 6 SERVINGS

1 Tbsp (15 mL) butter
1 Tbsp (15 mL) olive oil
2 lb (900 g) stewing beef, cut into 1-inch (2.5 cm) cubes
2 cups (500 mL) finely diced carrots
1½ cups (375 mL) finely diced onions
1 cup (250 mL) diced celery
3½ cups (875 mL) canned diced tomatoes
1¼ cups (310 mL) tomato soup
1 Tbsp (15 mL) dried parsley flakes
1 tsp (5 mL) sugar
1 tsp (5 mL) salt
¼ tsp (1 mL) freshly ground pepper
¼ tsp (1 mL) dried thyme
8 cups (2 L) beef broth
2 beef bouillon cubes
2 cups (500 mL) diced peeled potatoes
½ cup (125 mL) pearl barley

ONE-POT MEALS

CORNED BEEF AND CABBAGE
Bouilli au Chou et à la Viande Salée

MAKES 4 TO 6 SERVINGS

3 lb (1.3 kg) corned beef
2 onions, peeled and
   quartered
2 tsp (10 mL) fresh whole
   peppercorns
2 bay leaves
1 medium white cabbage,
   cored and quartered
6 potatoes, peeled and
   quartered
1 turnip, peeled and cut into
   2-inch (5 cm) chunks
4 carrots, peeled and cut into
   2-inch (5 cm) chunks

LA VIANDE SALÉE (or corned beef) was an excellent way to preserve meat for the winter. Because the beef is brined in a heavy salt solution it is extremely important that you do not skip the initial boil and rinse. While it does take extra time, it's the difference between a very tasty and enjoyable meal and one that is not consumable.

In a large pot, cover corned beef with cold water, bring to a boil, and cook for 1 hour. Drain liquid and wash the pot to remove any salt residue. Return beef to the pot. Add onions, peppercorns, and bay leaves. Layer cabbage, potatoes, turnip, and carrots on top of the beef. Cover with water and bring to a boil, reduce heat, and simmer for 1 hour.

Remove pot from heat and use a slotted spoon to remove vegetables; set aside. Remove corned beef and slice it against the grain. Arrange sliced beef and vegetables on a platter. Discard water, onions, peppercorns, and bay leaves.

 Corned beef is commonly served with yellow mustard, lots of butter, and freshly ground pepper.

WINTER VEGETABLE PORK STEW
Ragoût de Porc et de Légumes d'Hiver

OVER THE CENTURIES, most Acadian families raised their own pigs over the summer and then slaughtered them in the fall. From the pig they would make boudin, *tête fromager* (head cheese), sausages, creton, and etouffee to get them through the winter. Pork stew was a family favourite and was eaten more often than beef stew. My own family didn't raise pork, which might be a good thing as I love meat but have a feeling that the pigs might have become pets.

In a Dutch oven, sauté smoked pork belly in vegetable oil over high heat. Once the fat has rendered, add pork shoulder and sear until brown; sprinkle with flour and mix to coat. Add onion and sauté until translucent, then add carrots, parsnips, turnip, potatoes, bay leaves, parsley, thyme, salt, and freshly ground pepper and stir. Once mixed together, add Dijon mustard, top with water or vegetable broth, and allow to boil for 20 minutes. Cover, reduce heat to medium, and let simmer for 2 hours, stirring occasionally.

MAKES 4 TO 6 SERVINGS

1 lb (450 g) smoked pork belly, cut into 1-inch (2.5 cm) squares

3 lb (1.3 kg) pork shoulder, cut into 1-inch (2.5 cm) squares

¼ cup (60 mL) all-purpose flour

1 medium onion, finely diced

4 medium carrots, peeled and chopped

3 medium parsnips, peeled and chopped

1 turnip, peeled and chopped

6 medium potatoes (skin on), chopped

2 bay leaves

2 sprigs fresh parsley

2 sprigs thyme

1 tsp (5 mL) salt

½ tsp (2 mL) freshly ground pepper

1 Tbsp (15 mL) Dijon mustard

6 cups (1.5 L) water or vegetable broth

POUTINE RÂPÉE

POUTINE RÂPÉE IS an Acadian custom famous in the New Brunswick area. What made this version of rappie pie unique was that it was steamed or boiled in the form of a ball and usually stuffed with salt pork. Potatoes were a staple and this was, for sure, a very creative way to use them. This is a custom that is still used today in many villages.

Grate potatoes with a fine cheese grater, place in a cheese cloth, and squeeze to remove all excess starch and water.

In a large bowl, add grated dried potatoes and salt to mashed potatoes and form into a ball roughly the size of a tennis ball. Make a hole in the centre of the ball and add 1 Tbsp (15 mL) of chopped salt pork; reform and roll in flour, remove excess flour, and set aside. Continue until all of the potatoes are gone.

Bring a good-sized pot of water to boil. Submerge the balls in water, return to a boil, and simmer for 2 to 2½ hours. Remove from the pot and serve with your favourite side, such as molasses, brown sugar, white sugar, maple syrup, or even butter.

 To remove excess starch and water, it was not uncommon to place potatoes in a clean pillowcase, tie it, and place it in the spin cycle of the washer.

Some salt pork may need to be soaked overnight and rinsed.

MAKES 4 TO 6 DUMPLINGS

2 lb (900 g) raw potatoes, peeled and grated

1 Tbsp (15 mL) salt

4 cups (1 L) mashed potatoes (no cream or butter)

4 to 6 Tbsp (60 to 90 mL) finely chopped salt pork

3 Tbsp (45 mL) all-purpose flour

WINE BRAISED BEEF STEW
Ragoût de Bœuf Braisé au Vin

MAKES 4 TO 6 SERVINGS

2 lb (900 g) stewing beef, cut into 1 to 1½-inch (2.5 to 4 cm) cubes
¼ cup (60 mL) all-purpose flour
¼ cup (60 mL) vegetable oil
1 Tbsp (15 mL) butter
3 cloves garlic, chopped
1 medium onion, finely diced
2 sticks celery, finely diced
1 Tbsp (15 mL) Dijon mustard
1 tsp (5 mL) salt
½ tsp (2 mL) freshly ground pepper
2 sprigs fresh thyme
3 cups (750 mL) red wine
5 cups (1.25 L) beef broth
2 bay leaves
4 potatoes, peeled and cubed
4 carrots, peeled and chopped
1 medium turnip, peeled and cut into chunks

NOTHING SAYS COMFORT like the aroma of stew on a crisp fall day. Acadians are well versed in using the tougher cuts of meat, such as stewing beef, but they also know that using the proper cooking method will produce beef that's tender and juicy. This recipe uses a braising method and is finished in the oven. It relies on wine for depth of flavour and I like to use the same wine that I'll be serving with the meal.

Preheat oven to 350°F (175°C).

Dredge beef in flour. Heat oil in a Dutch oven on a medium-high heat; add the beef and brown in batches, being mindful not to over crowd the pan. Add more oil if necessary. Remove all beef from the pot.

Add butter to the pot and sauté garlic, onion, and celery until they begin to soften. Add Dijon mustard, salt, freshly ground pepper, and thyme. Combine then deglaze with red wine, scraping up all the browned bits from the bottom. Add beef, beef broth, and bay leaves. Cover and bring to a boil for 5 minutes.

Place Dutch oven in the preheated oven for 30 minutes. Remove and add potatoes, carrots, and turnip, then return to the oven for another 60 minutes.

 If time permits, make the stew the day before. Letting your stew sit overnight will enhance its flavours.

RAPPIE PIE
Râpure

RECIPE BY CHEF PAUL THIMOT, NOVA SCOTIA
COMMUNITY COLLEGE

MAKES 4 TO 6 SERVINGS

One 5- to 6-lb (2.25 to 2.75 kg)
stewing hen (or chicken;
bone in, skin on)
2 medium onions, diced into
1-inch (2.5 cm) pieces
2 Tbsp (30 mL) herbes salées
(see page 173)
10 lb (4.5 kg) starchy potatoes
(such as russets)
Chicken stock (amount varies,
see method)
Freshly ground pepper to taste
Salt to taste

WHEN IT COMES to rappie pie, there are grounds for an all-out Acadian dispute from one end of L'Acadie to the other. The verdict is out on whose version is the best—some love it runny, some love it firm, and some just don't like it at all. For this recipe, I called upon a chef friend, Paul Thimot, from the Annapolis Valley of Nova Scotia to help me out—his rappie pie is the best I have ever tasted.

Preheat oven to 400°F (200°C).

In a large pot, add stewing hen with diced onions, herbes salées, and enough water to cover. Simmer for 1 hour or until you can pull meat from the chicken bones. Remove hen and reserve the broth. Let the chicken cool until you can easily tear the meat into bite-sized pieces. Refrigerate meat and return bones to the cooking pot with the reserved broth. Simmer broth for another 3 to 4 hours then strain the bones out. This can be done a day ahead. Refrigerate if not using immediately.

Peel and finely grate potatoes; use a cloth bag to squeeze as much water as you can from them (measure how much water is removed, as this is how much chicken broth you will need to replace later). In a medium pot, add prepared chicken broth equivalent to the amount of water removed from the potatoes and bring to a boil. Add grated potatoes and mix together with either a potato masher or a whisk. Season with freshly ground pepper and salt.

Pour half the potato mixture into a greased 9- × 13-inch (23 × 33 cm) pan. Top with chicken meat and layer with the remaining potato mixture to cover the chicken. Place in the oven and bake for 3 hours or until a firm golden brown crust forms.

 You can use a juicer that saves pulp to prepare the potatoes. Simply wash, peel, and feed through the juicer, remembering to measure the juice extracted as it will need to be replaced with chicken stock.

BERNARD'S POT ROAST WITH POTATOES
Rôti de Patates à Bernard

WE GREW UP eating pot roast cooked this way. It has always been called Bernard's Pot Roast, although oddly enough there is no one in my family that knows who Bernard is! This isn't your typical pot roast as it is not meant to be cooked and sliced but rather shredded then put back in its juices along with the potatoes. It was always served with ployes (see page 184) for soaking up the juices and if Bernard is out there somewhere, I salute you!

Preheat oven to 350°F (175°C).

In a roasting pan over high heat, melt butter and sear beef on all sides (locking in juices). Add onions and sauté until they start to become translucent. Remove pan from burner and add carrots, water, salt, and freshly ground pepper. Cover and cook in the oven for 2½ hours. Uncover and cook for an additional 30 minutes. Remove from oven and let rest for 15 minutes. Remove roast and set aside on a plate; tent with foil paper.

Place pot back on a medium-high burner and add potatoes. Cover with water and cook until potatoes are fork tender—they will turn brown from the beef drippings and water will reduce. While potatoes are cooking, shred beef and, just before potatoes are completely cooked, incorporate the beef back into the pot to keep it moist. On a serving tray or platter, combine the potatoes, juices, and beef. Serve.

MAKES 4 TO 6 SERVINGS

1 Tbsp (15 mL) butter
3 lb (1.3 kg) roast beef (use a fatty cut such as a shoulder)
2 onions, julienned
3 carrots, peeled and cut into chunks
3 cups (750 mL) water
1 tsp (5 mL) salt
½ tsp (2 mL) freshly ground pepper
8 potatoes, peeled and cut in half

RAPPIE PIE, PEI STYLE
Râpure de l'Ile-du-Prince-Édouard

MAKES 8 SERVINGS

5 lb (2.25 kg) raw potatoes, peeled
2½ cups (625 mL) mashed potatoes
1 cup (250 mL) vegetable oil
1 lb (450 g) double-smoked bacon, cooked and chopped (see note)
Freshly ground pepper to taste

ON PRINCE EDWARD ISLAND, rappie pie is served much firmer than it is elsewhere. The inspiration for this recipe came from my friend Brenda Rogers, and it was passed down to her from her grandmother, Edna Arsenault, who recently passed away at the tender age of 103. This recipe is served daily at the Centre Expo-Festival in Abrams Village, and I use it on a regular basis because it is so firm and easy to eat.

Preheat oven to 350°F (175°C).

Finely grate potatoes and rinse in cold water, squeezing out as much water as possible.

In a large bowl, combine the grated potatoes with mashed potatoes, vegetable oil, bacon, and freshly ground pepper. Firmly press mixture into a greased 9- × 13-inch (23 × 33 cm) pan and bake for 3 hours, or until crust is golden brown.

 Cooked pork roast, baked ham, or chicken can be used in place of the bacon.

SPRING HODGE PODGE
Bouilli de Printemps

ONCE SPRING HAS sprung there is no better way to celebrate than with old-fashioned hodge podge. After a long winter, there is nothing better than eating veggies straight from the garden, cooked up in butter and cream. "Hodge podge" means a mixture of everything, so feel free to use whatever you have on hand or find at your local farmer's market.

Wash vegetables and trim ends off the beans and peas. In a large pot, bring 4 cups (1 L) water to a boil. Add beans, peas, carrots, and potatoes then cover, return to a boil, reduce heat to medium, and cook vegetables until fork tender, about 25 minutes.

Meanwhile, in a small saucepan, bring cream and butter to just below boiling; whisk in flour and continue to stir until slightly thickened. Drain vegetables, reserving 2 cups (500 mL) of the cooking liquid. Add cooking liquid to the cream mixture and pour overtop of the vegetables. Garnish with green onions.

MAKES 2 TO 4 SERVINGS

1 cup (250 mL) green beans
1 cup (250 mL) yellow beans
1 cup (250 mL) sugar snap
   peas
2 cups (500 mL) baby carrots
2 lb (900 g) new potatoes
1 cup (250 mL) cream (35%)
¼ cup (60 mL) butter
2 tsp (10 mL) all-purpose flour
16 green onions, chopped

SLOW COOKER BAKED BEANS
Fèves au Lard

BAKED BEANS WERE a traditional Saturday night supper for many decades. All the kids were home from school, Dad was home from work, and Mom was catching up with the week's chores. It was convenient to throw this meal together in the bean crock in the morning and let the oven slowly do its magic. This updated version uses a slow cooker so it's the same principle, you get to enjoy the day and come home to a classic dinner.

Rinse white beans and soak overnight in cold water. Rinse beans again, cover with fresh water, and place on the stove. Bring to a boil, then reduce heat and simmer for 30 minutes. Drain and reserve 4 cups (1 L) bean water; set aside. In the bottom of a slow cooker, place onion slices and top with beans. In a medium bowl, combine vinegar, brown sugar, garlic, dry mustard, baking soda, molasses, barbeque sauce, salt, and freshly ground pepper; mix well and pour over the beans, mixing to combine. Add the bean water to the slow cooker and arrange bacon pieces on top. Cover and cook on low for 7 hours. Remove 1 cup (250 mL) beans, mash, and stir back in. Cook, uncovered, for half an hour on high. Beans freeze very well.

Serve these beans with Homemade Bread (see page 189).

MAKES 8 TO 10 SERVINGS

2 lb (900 g) dried white beans
1 large onion, sliced
2 tsp (10 mL) cider vinegar
1 Tbsp (15 mL) brown sugar
2 cloves garlic, grated
½ tsp (2 mL) dry mustard
½ tsp (2 mL) baking soda
¼ cup (60 mL) molasses
1 cup (250 mL) barbeque
    sauce
1 Tbsp (15 mL) salt
2 tsp (10 mL) freshly ground
    pepper
4 cups (1 L) boiling water
2 oz (60 g) double-smoked
    bacon, cooked and chopped
    into 1-inch (2.5 cm) pieces

BEEF CHIARD
Chiard au Boeuf

MAKES 4 SERVINGS

1 Tbsp (15 mL) butter

1 lb (450 g) stewing beef, cut
in ½-inch (1 cm) cubes

1 large onion, diced

½ tsp (2 mL) salt

½ tsp (2 mL) freshly ground
pepper

2 cups (500 mL) water + extra
to cover

6 to 8 potatoes, peeled and
sliced

2 to 3 carrots, diced

1 tsp (5 mL) herbes salées
(see page 173)

A CHIARD IS really a quick traditional Acadian dish sometimes called a "pot de chiard." It loosely translates to "a mess of food," but don't be fooled—this traditional dish is tasty. It is often made from beef, but depending of the area it is sometimes made with bologna, hot dogs, or just plain potatoes and onions.

Melt butter in a heavy bottomed pot on high heat and sauté beef cubes, onion, salt, and freshly ground pepper for 3 to 5 minutes, or until beef is brown on all sides. Add 2 cups (500 mL) water and simmer until tender, about 1 hour. Add potatoes and carrots and enough water to cover; add herbes salées. Bring to a boil, stir occasionally, then simmer until potatoes start to fall apart and there is very little water left.

If substituting hot dogs or bologna for the beef, cook for only few minutes (instead of the hour required for beef) before adding the potatoes.

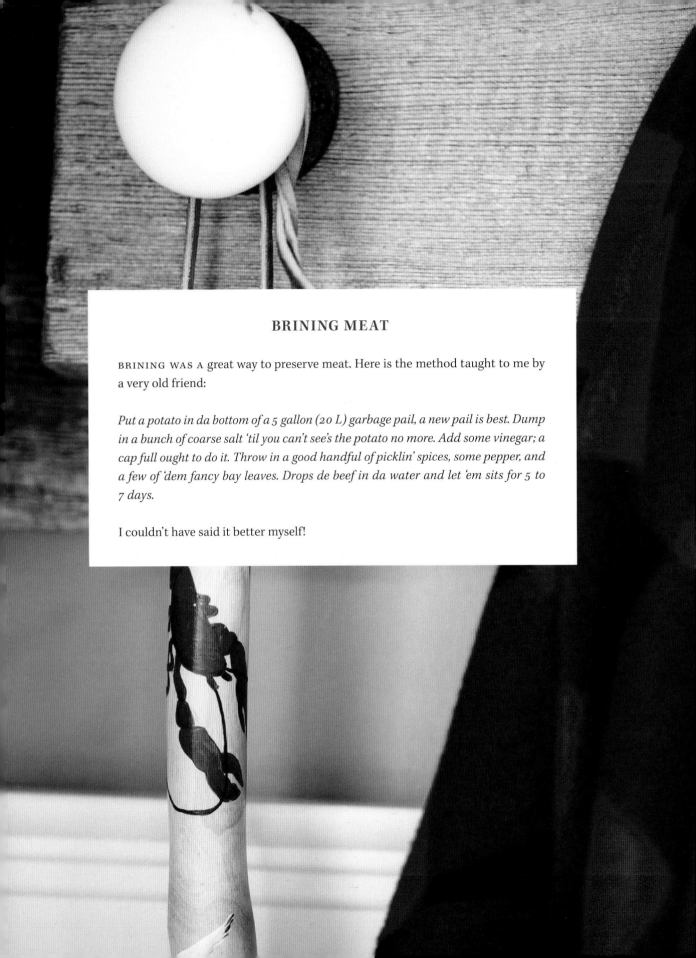

BRINING MEAT

BRINING WAS A great way to preserve meat. Here is the method taught to me by a very old friend:

Put a potato in da bottom of a 5 gallon (20 L) garbage pail, a new pail is best. Dump in a bunch of coarse salt 'til you can't see's the potato no more. Add some vinegar; a cap full ought to do it. Throw in a good handful of picklin' spices, some pepper, and a few of 'dem fancy bay leaves. Drops de beef in da water and let 'em sits for 5 to 7 days.

I couldn't have said it better myself!

FALL BOILED DINNER
Bouilli d'Automne

BOILED DINNER CAN be made with ham or beef, and this meal requires very little work beyond preparing the vegetables. My mom usually made it when we were at the cottage, usually in late August or early September. I was always a little sad to see boiled dinner on the table because it signaled the end of summer and the end of cottage season.

In a large stock pot, place ham, potatoes, corn, beans, carrots, parsnips, onions, turnip, and bouquet garni; cover with cold water. Place over high heat, cover, and bring to a boil. Reduce heat to a slow boil and allow to cook for 1 hour to 1½ hours, or until meat is tender. The vegetables will be very soft and ham will fall off the bone. Drain liquid and serve with butter, salt, freshly ground pepper, and mustard.

Most bouquet garni should consist of 3 sprigs fresh parsley, 1 bay leaf, 1 clove peeled garlic, and 4 black peppercorns tied together in cheesecloth with kitchen twine.

MAKES 4 TO 6 SERVINGS

2 lb (900 g) ham (bone in)
8 large potatoes, peeled and halved
8 ears of corn, cut into thirds
1 lb (450 g) green beans, ends trimmed
4 carrots, cut into quarters
3 parsnips, peeled and cut into quarters
2 yellow onions, peeled and cut into quarters
1 large turnip, peeled and cubed
1 bouquet garni (see note)
Butter, for serving
Salt, for serving
Freshly ground pepper, for serving
Mustard to taste (heat level and variety are up to you)

ENTRÉES FROM THE SEA

SALT FISH AND POTATO DINNER WITH EGG SAUCE | *Repas de Morue Salée et Pommes de Terre Nappées de Sauce aux Oeufs* 84

SAVOURY SALT COD CAKES | *Beignets de Morue Salée* 86

GRILLED SALMON FILET WITH A CITRUS EGG SAUCE | *Filet de Saumon Grillé Nappé d'une Sauce aux Oeufs et aux Agrumes* 88

LOBSTER BOIL | *Homard Bouilli* 91

LOBSTER ROLL | *Guédille au Homard* 95

HADDOCK WITH A CREAMED LOBSTER SAUCE | *Aiglefin Nappé d'une Sauce Crémeuse au Homard* 96

SEAFOOD PIE | *Pâté aux Fruits de Mer* 99

FRIED SMELTS | *Éperlan Frit* 100

STEAMER CLAMS | *Palourdes Cuites à la Vapeur* 101

SALT FISH AND POTATO DINNER WITH EGG SAUCE

Repas de Morue Salée et Pommes de Terre Nappées de Sauce aux Oeufs

MAKES 4 SERVINGS

1 lb (450 g) salt cod or any other salted white fish

1 lb (450 g) uncooked bacon, cut into ½-inch (1 cm) pieces

4 large potatoes, peeled and quartered

Egg Sauce, for serving (recipe follows)

FOR CENTURIES, SALTING cod was a way of life if you lived near the water. It was a simple method to preserve fish for the winter. The salt as well as other fish were served mostly with potatoes to help break the saltiness and both were plentiful. The most common way was to simply boil the fish and serve it with a simple sauce; the recipe below has been around for centuries and is still a favourite today.

In a large pot filled with water, add salt cod, cover, and soak overnight. Change water in the morning and continue soaking. Before cooking, empty half of the water and replace with fresh water. Put the pot on the stove, bring to a boil, and cook for 10 to 15 minutes.

In a frying pan, fry bacon until crisp. Set aside. In a pot of water, boil potatoes, drain, and set aside.

To serve, place potatoes on a serving dish, top with fish, sprinkle with bacon, and top with Egg Sauce.

EGG SAUCE

MAKES 1⅓ CUPS (330 ML)

2 Tbsp (30 mL) butter

2 Tbsp (30 mL) all-purpose flour

1 cup (250 mL) whole milk

2 tsp (10 mL) yellow prepared mustard

Salt to taste

Freshly ground pepper to taste

2 hard-boiled eggs, chopped pea size

To prepare egg sauce, melt butter in a medium saucepan, add flour, and cook, stirring constantly, until golden brown. Add milk and mustard and heat until thick, stirring continuously. Season with salt and freshly ground pepper and fold in boiled eggs.

SALTING FISH

SALTING WAS A method of preserving fish and meat for winter that is still used today. The first step in salting fish is preparing the fish itself. Start by removing the head, gills, and guts, and giving it a good rinse in sea water (if possible). Remove all traces of blood and membranes, and remove all the scales. Butterfly the fish, removing the spine but leaving the skin around the spine intact.

Find a large container and layer the bottom with coarse salt. Add a layer of fish with the flesh side exposed, cover with salt, then continue the process until the container is full. The top layer should be a salt layer.

After a few hours, the fish will begin to release its natural liquids and a brine will have been created. Keep the fish immersed in the brine at room temperature, allowing 24 hours for each 1 inch (2.5 cm) of thickness in the flesh.

Store in a dry cool space until needed.

The drying of salt fish is the same process, except that after butterflying the fish you lay it on racks made from spruce branches to air dry. Sprinkle coarse salt on the fish and let it sit until hard and dry.

SAVOURY SALT COD CAKES
Beignets de Morue Salée

MAKES 4 SERVINGS

1 lb (450 g) salt cod
¼ cup (60 mL) finely diced
  celery
1 large onion, chopped
2½ cups (625 mL) mashed
  potatoes
1 Tbsp (15 mL) summer savory
1 tsp (5 mL) freshly ground
  pepper
1 egg, beaten
¼ cup (60 mL) all-purpose
  flour
2 Tbsp (30 mL) vegetable oil

SALTING COD IS a tradition that goes far back in Acadian culture, and it was very common to see racks of salted cod drying up and down the shore. Salt cod was a staple in every home and was relied on to help sustain an Acadian family through the long winter. It was not uncommon for fish cakes to make an appearance on the dining table at least once a day, seven days a week.

In a medium bowl, cover salt cod with cold fresh water. Soak for 3 hours.

Drain and rinse cod with fresh water. In a medium saucepan, add cod, celery, and onion; top with cold water and bring to gentle boil. Cook until fork tender, about 8 to 10 minutes, then drain.

In a large bowl, add mashed potatoes, cod mixture, and summer savory; mix well. Stir in freshly ground pepper and egg, then refrigerate mixture for 30 minutes to firm up. Remove from refrigerator and form into 3-oz (90 g) patties; lightly dredge in flour. Heat oil in a skillet over medium-high heat and fry patties in oil on both sides until golden.

 Traditionally cod cakes are served with a side of tomato chow (see page 162) or mustard pickles (see page 163).

GRILLED SALMON FILET WITH A CITRUS EGG SAUCE

Filet de Saumon Grillé Nappé d'une Sauce aux Oeufs et aux Agrumes

MAKES 4 SERVINGS

Four 6- to 8-oz (175 to 235 g) salmon filets
Salt to taste
Freshly ground pepper to taste
2 Tbsp (30 mL) vegetable oil
Citrus Egg Sauce, for serving (recipe follows)

TO DRESS UP a common fish dish or elevate it to company status, an egg sauce was often served alongside. This was most common with salmon or trout.

Season the salmon filets with salt and freshly ground pepper. In a cast iron pan, heat the oil; once it starts to sizzle add the salmon filets and sear on each side for 2 minutes. Remove filets from the burner and finish in an oven for 10 to 12 minutes. Serve with Citrus Egg Sauce.

CITRUS EGG SAUCE

MAKES 3 CUPS (750 ML)

2 Tbsp (30 mL) butter
½ cup (125 mL) diced green onions
2 Tbsp (30 mL) all-purpose flour
1½ cups (375 mL) whole milk
½ cup (125 mL) cream (35%)
¼ cup (60 mL) white wine
3 hard-boiled eggs, diced
½ lemon, juiced
Salt to taste
Freshly ground pepper to taste

Melt butter in a heavy bottomed pot over medium-high heat, add onions, and sauté. Slowly whisk in flour and stir until it begins to thicken. Let it sweat a bit, then incorporate milk, cream, and white wine. Keep stirring until the sauce reduces by a third. Lightly fold in cooked eggs and lemon juice. Finish with salt and freshly ground pepper to taste.

LOBSTER BOIL
Homard Bouilli

IF YOU LIVED by the sea, lobster was a dietary staple and always plentiful. Acadian children who grew up with a father that fished lobsters often took lobster sandwiches to school for lunch, where it would take work to trade up to a peanut butter and jam sandwich! How times have changed.

This recipe will show you how to cook lobster Acadian style. We believe that the proper way to eat lobster is cold, dipped in hot butter, outside on a picnic table covered with newspaper alongside a great potato salad. If it is too cold outside, just move your lobster to the kitchen table.

Before cooking your lobster, always remove rubber bands, as the rubber taste can permeate the meat. Fill a very large stock pot with water and add salt (1 cup/250 mL for every 4 cups/1 L water). Bring to a boil, add lobsters, cover, and boil for 12 to 14 minutes. Once you add the lobsters to the pot the water temperature will drop, so count your minutes from the time that the water returns to a boil. Once cooked, remove lobsters from the pot and submerge in an ice bath to halt the cooking process, about 4 to 5 minutes or until cool to the touch. (Alternatively, you can steam lobsters: in a pot, add 2 to 3 inches/5 to 8 cm of boiling salted water, add lobsters, cover, and steam for 11 to 13 minutes.)

Once lobster is cooled, remove it from the ice bath and place it on its back in a storage bin at bottom of the fridge. This keeps the juices in and allows the meat to remain moist. Cover the lobster with damp newspaper. Lobster should be eaten within 2 to 3 days.

 Potato salad to accompany lobster can be found on page 174.

MAKES 6 SERVINGS

Six 1¼- to 1½-lb (560 to 680 g) live lobsters
Salt to taste

CRACKING A COOKED LOBSTER

TWIST THE TAIL To remove the tail, grasp the lobster around the body with one hand and the tail with the other and gently twist. Pull apart the two pieces.

CUT OR CRACK OPEN THE TAIL To remove the meat from the tail, squeeze both sides together until you hear (feel) the shell crack. Grab each side of the tail with a hand and open like a book. The meat can now be easily removed.

TWIST THE CLAWS To remove the claws, simply grab the body with one hand and gently twist the claws and knuckle with the other. Both claws and knuckles will separate easily from the body. Use care when holding the knuckle as it has sharp protrusions that can hurt if not handled carefully.

CUT OR CRACK THE CLAWS OPEN Crack the claws open with a sharp heavy knife, or use a lobster cracker (like a nut cracker). Simply bend the claw after it is cracked and the meat can easily be extracted. You can also use the cracker to break the knuckle shell. Don't forget to remove the meat found in the small part of the lower claws . . . you will want to get every tasty morsel.

LEGS AND BODY The legs and the body also contain edible meat. Break and open the legs at the joint and use a fork or skewer to draw out the slender pieces of meat contained inside. For the body, simply pull apart the shell to expose the meat. Remember that all of the lobster, aside from the part located behind the eyes, is edible, and the choice is up to you how much you wish to eat.

 You may notice a green substance on the meat which is called the tomalley. There may also be a red substance known as the roe (eggs) found in some female lobster. Both are edible and considered by many to be one of their favourite parts. However, they can be scraped off if desired.

DE-BUNKING A FEW COMMON LOBSTER MYTHS:

- Lobsters do not scream when they are submerged in water; they have no vocal cords. The noise you hear is air escaping from their lungs. My theory is that Mom and Dad were in cahoots—if the kids thought that the poor lobsters were crying out then maybe they wouldn't have any, leaving more for the adults!

- We were always told that if you drank milk while eating lobster you could get at least an upset stomach, and at worst it could lead to gout. I never questioned this until one day when I was sitting down enjoying a bowl of chowder.

- Some people say that hard shell lobster is better than soft shell—that's really a matter of personal choice.

- Lobster are not endangered. The fishery conservation and management system in Atlantic. Canada is regarded as one of the most stringent and sophisticated in the world.

- Atlantic Canada produces more lobster than the entire USA, and it's available fresh all year round!

LOBSTER ROLL
Guédille au Homard

THE GUÉDILLE IS our version of a lobster roll, and it's very similar to a traditional lobster roll. After the Second World War, when lobster was expensive, it was a treat reserved for special occasions and, to make it stretch further, there was often more iceberg lettuce than lobster in the roll. Unlike traditional lobster rolls, the lettuce in a Guédille is mixed in with the filling rather than placed on top. A Guédille was a very common way to eat lobster, and you'll still find them on canteen menus throughout Acadian country. It was one of my Dad's favourite meals and it's still very nostalgic for me.

Butter hot dog buns on both sides (outsides), place in a frying pan over medium heat, and grill until each side is golden. In a bowl, mix lobster meat, celery, mayonnaise, salt, and freshly ground pepper. Add iceberg lettuce and mix well. Divide filling between buns.

 Serve with potato chips or homemade French fries.

MAKES 4 LOBSTER ROLLS

4 hot dog buns
2 Tbsp (30 mL) butter, softened
½ lb (250 g) lobster meat, chopped
2 Tbsp (30 mL) diced celery
1½ Tbsp (22 mL) mayonnaise
Pinch of salt
Pinch of freshly ground pepper
½ head of iceberg lettuce, shredded

HADDOCK WITH A CREAMED LOBSTER SAUCE

Aiglefin Nappé d'une Sauce Crémeuse au Homard

MAKES 4 SERVINGS

CREAMED LOBSTER SAUCE

3 Tbsp (45 mL) butter, divided
1 lb (450 g) cooked lobster
    meat, finely chopped
1 Tbsp (15 mL) white vinegar
½ cup (125 mL) heavy cream
    (35%)
¼ cup (60 mL) light cream
    (18%)
1 Tbsp (15 mL) chopped chives

PAN FRIED HADDOCK

1 cup (250 mL) all-purpose
    flour
2 eggs, beaten
Pinch of salt
Pinch of freshly ground pepper
Four 8-oz (235 g) haddock
    fillets
1 Tbsp (15 mL) butter

FRESH SEAFOOD HAS always been in abundance since the Acadians arrived in eastern Canada, and creamed lobster is a dish that is synonymous with the South Shore of Nova Scotia. Often the fishermen would prepare and eat this dish on the lobster boats; it is typically served on toast and can still be found in restaurants all over the region. Haddock and cod would also have been in abundance, and combining the two seemed to make perfect sense.

In a frying pan, melt 2 Tbsp (30 mL) butter, add lobster meat, and fry until lobster becomes bright red and begins to pop and sizzle in the pan. Add vinegar and cook until vinegar is almost gone. Add remaining 1 Tbsp (15 mL) butter, heavy cream, light cream, and chives; reduce for a minute or two. Set aside.

Place flour in a shallow dish. In a second shallow dish, mix together eggs, salt, and freshly ground pepper. Roll fish fillets in flour then dip in the egg mixture. In a large cast iron pan, melt butter and cook 2 fillets at a time, 2 to 3 minutes on each side or until golden brown. Add more butter if needed. Place fish in a low-temperature oven until ready to serve; warm sauce and drape over the fish.

 This recipe is also really good using cod instead of lobster.

SEAFOOD PIE
Pâté aux Fruits de Mer

SEAFOOD PIE IS a staple Acadian dish that was eaten whenever seafood was in abundance. I love serving it for brunch with a green salad.

Preheat oven to 350°F (175°C).

On a floured surface, roll out two 9-inch (23 cm) pie crusts. Place the first pie crust in a deep 9-inch (23 cm) pie plate and set aside.

In a small pot, boil potatoes until fork tender. Drain and set aside.

Place Béchamel Sauce in a heavy bottomed pot. Add lobster, snow crab, coldwater shrimp, potatoes, Gruyère, and parmesan cheese and bring to a simmer. Once hot, pour seafood mixture into the pie crust, add chives, and cover with the second pie crust. Crimp edges together and cut small slits in the middle of the pie to allow steam to vent. Place on a cookie sheet and bake for 35 to 40 minutes, or until pie is golden brown. Let cool for 10 minutes then serve.

MAKES 4 TO 6 SERVINGS

- 2 lb (900 g) Savoury Pie Dough (enough for two 9-inch/23-cm pie crusts; see page 186)
- 2 potatoes, peeled and diced
- 2 cups (500 mL) Béchamel Sauce (recipe follows)
- ½ lb (250 g) lobster meat
- ¼ lb (115 g) snow crab or rock crab
- ½ lb (250 g) coldwater shrimp
- ½ cup (125 mL) shredded Gruyère
- ¼ cup (60 mL) grated parmesan cheese
- 3 chives, diced

BÉCHAMEL SAUCE

In a heavy bottomed pot on medium-high heat, melt butter and sauté onions until translucent. Slowly whisk in flour until it starts to become stiff; let it sweat for a few minutes. Incorporate milk and continue to stir while the sauce reduces. Remove from heat, add white wine, and pass ingredients through a strainer.

MAKES 2 CUPS (500 ML)

- 2 Tbsp (30 mL) butter
- ½ cup (125 mL) diced onion
- 2 Tbsp (30 mL) all-purpose flour
- 2 cups (500 mL) milk
- ¼ cup (60 mL) white wine

FRIED SMELTS
Éperlan Frit

MAKES 2 TO 4 SERVINGS

1 lb (450 g) smelts
½ cup (125 mL) all-purpose
   flour
1 tsp (5 mL) salt
5 Tbsp (75 mL) lard or butter

AS A KID, there wasn't anything more fun than spending a day on the lake or river fishing smelts. The ice was cut, lines went in, and there was lots of time to tell tall tales and fishing stories. Smelts are now fished commercially, but for centuries it was a way for many people to get fresh fish in the winter and for some to subsidize their incomes. Usually dusted in all-purpose flour or cornmeal and fried, smelts are always a treat. Smelt fries are commonly eaten today by many in small Acadian villages as the centerpiece of a well-loved social gathering.

Clean smelts by removing the head and innards, then wipe dry. In a shallow bowl, combine flour and salt. Roll smelts in flour, shaking off the excess. In a heavy bottomed frying pan over medium-high heat, melt lard or butter. Cook the cut side (stomach) of the smelts first, then cook the other 2 sides until golden brown, about 2 to 3 minutes per side. Wipe pan between each batch and add clean lard or butter to avoid black crumbs sticking to the fish.

 You can serve with white vinegar if you like.

STEAMER CLAMS
Palourdes Cuites à la Vapeur

DIGGING FOR SOFT shell clams along the shore is a great way to spend quality family time. The trick is to look for little holes in the sand. These are the breathing holes—you scoop the sand around the hole away until the clam reveals itself. To make a truly memorable experience, cook the clams over an open flame directly on the beach—now that is the life!

Place all ingredients except butter into a pot and cover; turn burner to medium-high and cook until steam starts to barrel out from under the lid. Turn burner off and let clams sit in the pot for 2 to 3 minutes. In a small pot, melt butter over medium heat to serve alongside the clams for dipping.

MAKES 4 SERVINGS

5 lb (2.25 kg) soft shell clams
   (also known as little neck or
   steamer clams)
1 cup (250 mL) white wine
½ yellow onion, diced
2 sprigs parsley
¼ cup (60 mL) butter

ENTRÉES FROM THE FARM

SHEPHERD'S PIE BOSSÉ STYLE
Pâté Chinois de la Famille Bossé

MAKES 4 TO 6 SERVINGS

1 lb (450 g) lean ground beef

1 medium onion, diced

½ tsp (2 mL) salt + extra to taste

½ tsp (2 mL) freshly ground pepper + extra to taste

1 lb (450 g) potatoes, peeled and quartered

6 Tbsp (90 mL) butter, softened, divided

¼ cup (60 mL) heavy cream (35%)

One 14-oz (400 g) can creamed corn

SHEPHERD'S PIE IS a relatively new dish in the Acadian repertoire and like many "borrowed" dishes, Acadians have made it their own. My mom didn't use the usual carrots and peas, we ate it with creamed-style corn.

Preheat oven to 350°F (175°C).

In a medium frying pan on high heat, sauté beef; when browned, add onion, salt, and freshly ground pepper. Continue to cook until onions soften and there is no pink left in the beef. Set aside.

In a large pot, cover potatoes with water and boil until fork tender; drain, and add ¼ cup (60 mL) butter and cream. Mash until fluffy, season with salt and freshly ground pepper. Set aside.

Add ground beef mixture to the bottom of an 8- × 8-inch (20 × 20 cm) baking pan. Top with creamed corn then spread buttery mashed potatoes on top. Spread remaining 2 Tbsp (30 mL) butter over the top and bake for 45 minutes or until golden brown.

POTATOES IN LARD
Pommes de Terre au Lard

MAKES 4 SERVINGS

2 Tbsp (30 mL) lard, divided
6 to 8 potatoes (skin on),
   thinly sliced
½ tsp (2 mL) freshly ground
   pepper + extra to taste
1 small onion, finely chopped
4 eggs
2 Tbsp (30 mL) cream (35%)

PATATES DANS LA GRAISE or *grillade* are potatoes fried to a golden brown with crisp, curled edges—it doesn't get any better than that. This was always done in a cast iron skillet, and the lard is not optional! Often my Mom would cook the potatoes with some onions and then pour scrambled eggs on top. It is comfort food at its best. I make them about once a year, but I would eat them once a week if my heart could take it! This dish has been renamed Hangover Hash in our house as it's guaranteed to cure the "weekend flu."

In a good-sized frying pan (preferably cast iron), melt 1 Tbsp (15 mL) lard; add potatoes and freshly ground pepper. Be patient and allow potatoes to brown and crisp a bit before turning. Once turned, add the remaining lard and chopped onion; repeat cooking process, making sure that all potatoes are golden brown. This will take 15 to 20 minutes.

When potatoes are cooked, mix eggs with cream, add freshly ground pepper, and pour on top of the potatoes. Let eggs cook on the bottom, then flip. The onions will blacken a bit but this is normal and creates an amazing flavour.

 Using a cast iron frying pan will always give you the best results.

GRILLADE: COOKING ON THE CAST IRON STOVE

THE CAST IRON stove was used in every Acadian home probably up until the 1960s. The stove top was used daily to make toast—with a quick sweep of an old newspaper to the top of the stove to remove any dust and dirt. The key to toasting was to wait until bread was seared before turning.

A good hot stove was also the preferred way to make good ployes, and thinly sliced potatoes can be placed directly on to the stove to cook, which tastes great although the starch will leave marks on your stove (so make sure it's an old one). This was Acadia's version of French fries before they knew French fries even existed.

BEEF TONGUE SANDWICH
Sandwich de Langues de Boeuf

MAKES 4 SERVINGS

1 raw beef tongue
1 Tbsp (15 mL) coarse salt
8 slices sourdough bread
2 Tbsp (30 mL) butter
¼ cup (60 mL) mayonnaise
¼ cup (60 mL) Pickled Red
 Onions (recipe follows)
1 cup (250 mL) arugula
Freshly ground pepper to taste

THE BEEF TONGUE was never wasted when a cow was slaughtered. It was often one of the fall's most anticipated textures and flavours, used for making sandwiches to take in a lunch box by a hard-working person. Today, I make this sandwich with some more modern ingredients, including pickled onion, mayo, and arugula, served on a sourdough bun or hearty grain bread.

Wash and scrub the tongue and place in a large bowl. Thoroughly season with coarse salt, cover with water, and refrigerate overnight. The next day, rinse and cover with fresh water in a medium pot; bring to a boil then simmer until tender, about 1 hour. Remove from water, peel, and place on a plate to cool in the refrigerator.

Butter 1 side of each slice of bread and grill. Remove bread from the grill and spread the insides with mayonnaise. Remove tongue from refrigerator and cut into ¼-inch (0.5 cm) slices. Lay the meat evenly between the 4 sandwiches and top with pickled onions, arugula, and a few turns of the pepper mill. Cut sandwiches in half and wrap for a lunch box.

PICKLED RED ONIONS

MAKES 1½ CUPS (375 ML)

1 medium red onion, thinly
 sliced
½ cup (125 mL) white vinegar
½ cup (125 mL) water
1 bay leaf
1 tsp (5 mL) pickling spices

Place onion in a Mason jar. In a small pot, bring the rest of the ingredients to a boil, then pour on the onions. Cool in refrigerator for 1 hour before using.

CHICKEN POT PIE
Pâté au Poulet

FOR CENTURIES, CHICKEN pot pie has been the perfect way to use up leftover chicken or turkey. The chicken simmers with vegetables in a creamy sauce tucked under a savoury topping.

Preheat oven to 350°F (175°C).

In a large bowl, mix together flour, baking powder, salt, summer savory, and thyme. Grate in frozen butter. Use a fork to incorporate milk into the flour mixture, mixing just until the dough comes together. Roll out on a floured surface about 2 inches (5 cm) thick to fit a 9- × 13-inch (23 × 33 cm) baking dish. Set aside.

For the filling, melt butter in a large pot over medium heat. Add onion, potatoes, peas, celery, and carrot; sauté for 5 to 6 minutes. Mix flour with salt, summer savory, and thyme and add to the vegetables in the pan, stirring constantly; allow to brown but not burn. Add chicken stock, 1 cup (250 mL) at a time, stirring until thickened. Stir in chicken.

Turn filling out into a 9- × 13-inch (23 × 33 cm) baking dish, top with the biscuit mixture, and bake for 30 to 35 minutes or until the topping is golden brown and the filling is bubbly.

MAKES 6 TO 8 SERVINGS

BISCUIT TOPPING

2 cups (500 mL) all-purpose flour
1 Tbsp (15 mL) baking powder
1 tsp (5 mL) salt
¼ tsp (1 mL) summer savory
¼ tsp (1 mL) thyme
½ cup (125 mL) frozen butter
¾ cup (175 mL) milk

POT PIE FILLING

2 Tbsp (30 mL) butter
1 medium onion, finely diced
3 cups (750 mL) finely diced peeled potatoes
1 cup (250 mL) fresh peas (frozen will work as well)
½ cup (125 mL) finely diced celery
1 cup (250 mL) finely diced carrot
½ cup (125 mL) all-purpose flour
2 tsp (10 mL) salt
1 tsp (5 mL) summer savory
¼ tsp (1 mL) thyme
6 cups (1.5 L) chicken stock
12 oz (355 g) chicken meat, cooked and chopped

POTATO PANCAKES
Crêpes aux Pommes de Terre

MAKES 2 TO 4 SERVINGS

2 cups (500 mL) grated
    peeled potatoes
1 small onion, grated
2 eggs, beaten
¼ cup (60 mL) all-purpose
    flour
2 tsp (10 mL) salt
¼ cup (60 mL) finely chopped
    green onions
Caper Mayo, for garnish
    (recipe follows)

POTATO PANCAKES WERE often served as a side dish at home. We didn't have a fancy mayo to go with them, just a fancy "red" sauce, but I felt these needed a little something. If you're looking for a nice appetizer or light lunch, simply top with some smoked salmon and serve with a green salad.

Squeeze all moisture from the grated potatoes and place them in a medium bowl. Add onion and eggs and mix; add flour, salt, and green onions and mix well. In a large skillet, heat oil on high until it reaches its smoke point. Using heaping tablespoonfuls, drop potato mixture into the skillet and fry potato pancakes on each side until golden brown. Continue until all batter has been used. Remove pancakes to a plate lined with paper towels. Serve topped with Caper Mayo.

CAPER MAYO

MAKES ¾ CUP (175 ML)

¼ cup (60 mL) mayonnaise
¼ cup (60 mL) sour cream
1 Tbsp (15 mL) finely diced
    shallots
2 Tbsp (30 mL) capers,
    crushed
1 Tbsp (15 mL) lemon juice

In a small bowl, add mayonnaise, sour cream, shallots, capers, and lemon juice.

BLOOD PUDDING
Boudin du Pays

AT ONE TIME, almost every Acadian family would have made blood pudding each autumn, but it's an art that isn't practiced as much these days. It's highly labour intensive, and now that we are not all slaughtering our hogs in the fall we don't have the ingredients on hand. In Louisiana, white boudin is sold in every corner store and gas station and no two boudins are the same. See page 137 for a white boudin recipe.

Collect blood from a freshly slaughtered pig, add salt, and stir; this will prevent blood from congealing. Set aside.

Cut heart and neck into pieces. In a large heavy bottomed pot, render pork fat and brown pig heart and neck by searing meat on all sides; add onions and cover meat with water. Cover and simmer for 3 hours. Remove meat from pot and let cool; remove bones, then pass pork through a meat grinder twice so it's very fine. Add ground meat back to the cooking liquid along with spices. Return liquid to a boil. Strain blood through a cheese cloth and slowly add it to the mixture in the pot, stirring constantly. Add flour and make a slurry.

Fill a large pot halfway with water and bring to a boil, then reduce to a simmer. Tie a knot in one end of each sausage casing and use a funnel to fill with the meat mixture; tie off the top, leaving a few inches for expansion. Repeat with additional casings, then place the sausages in the hot water and cook for 1 hour, or until they start to float. Use a small needle to ensure that the sausages have firmed up and won't bleed out. Remove from hot water and pat dry, allow to rest and come to room temperature, then cool for 24 hours in refrigerator.

You can source sausage casings from your local butcher.

This recipe should be prepared at the time a pig is slaughtered to obtain the necessary ingredients.

MAKES 4 TO 6 COILS

1 gallon (4 L) pork blood
¼ cup (60 mL) salt
½ pig's heart
1 pigs neck
1 cup (250 mL) diced pork fat
4 onions, chopped
2 tsp (10 mL) freshly ground pepper
½ tsp (2 mL) ground cloves
½ tsp (2 mL) summer savory
½ tsp (2 mL) allspice
2 Tbsp (30 mL) all-purpose flour
4 to 6 natural sausage casings, cut 18 to 20 inches (45 to 50 cm) long

MEAT PIE
Pâté à la Viande

MAKES TWO 9-INCH (23 CM) PIES

FILLING

3 lb (1.3 kg) chicken thighs (bone in, skin on)
2 lb (900 g) pork roast
1 large onion, diced
1 Tbsp (15 mL) Kitchen Bouquet
Freshly ground pepper to taste
Salt to taste

CRUST

5 cups (1.25 L) all-purpose flour
1 tsp (5 mL) salt
5 tsp (25 mL) baking powder
1½ cups (375 mL) shortening
1 cup (250 mL) milk

I WANTED TO meet the best pie maker in the village of Cheticamp, New Brunswick, and Laurette Chiasson did not disappoint. She was kind enough to take the time to teach me how to make her famous meat pie. I loved it so much that I shared it with our readers in *Saltscapes* magazine, and now I share it with you (with Laurette's blessing, of course). Hugs and kisses Laurette. Your pâté à la viande is simply the best!

Preheat oven to 350°F (175°F).

Place all filling ingredients in a large roasting pan and cover with water. Cook on medium heat for 3 hours adding water as needed. When meat is cooked, remove from pot and reserve the broth. Once meat has cooled, remove any bones or fat and shred with a fork until the meat falls apart. Set aside.

In a large bowl, make the crust by mixing together flour, salt, baking powder, and shortening, making sure shortening is well incorporated. Add milk until you achieve a biscuit dough consistency; add more milk if dough is too dry.

On a flour-covered surface, roll out enough dough to cover the bottom of your pie plate. Add enough meat mixture to fill the pie plate just below the rim. Pour about ¼ cup (60 mL) reserved meat broth onto the meat mixture to keep meat moist during the baking process. Roll out enough dough to cover the pie, cutting off excess dough around the sides and making sure to cut out holes in the top of the pie crust so steam from the hot meat mixture can escape. Seal sides as desired. Repeat these same steps to make other pies. Bake for 30 to 35 minutes or until golden brown.

CHRISTMAS MEAT PIES

THE TYPICAL TIME to bake meat pies is at Christmas . . . it seems to just be something you must do. You shop for your meat, make sure you've purchased your large bag of flour and shortening, then count the pie plates! It can turn into a family activity pretty quick—cleaning the fat and bones from your meat, mixing the dough, rolling out the dough, filling the pie plates. The youngest ones are usually standing close by, ready to seal each pie with a fork and make a one-of-a-kind design. We would easily make anywhere from 10 to 30 meat pies, using some for gifts and saving the rest for the Christmas Eve get-togethers with family and friends. And don't forget Christmas morning breakfast! Before Christmas the usual chitchats among friends and family are not just about shopping, but asking one another if they've made their meat pies yet.

TOURTIÈRE

TOURTIÈRE IS A French tradition that was adopted into most Acadian homes and usually served for the Réveillon or during Christmas eve celebrations. At home we always served it with my mother's slaw (see page 28). I've introduced this tradition to many people and it's always well received.

I like to make my Tourtière in smaller, individual portions using a muffin pan. This particular recipe was inspired by Chef Jean Paul Grellier, who was my culinary school instructor many moons ago. Merci Chef!

Preheat oven to 375°F (190°C). In a large heavy bottomed pot, melt lard and sauté onions, garlic, pork, and veal until there is no pink left. Add beef broth, salt, freshly ground pepper, and allspice and let simmer for 1 hour.

In a small pot, boil potatoes until fork tender, drain water, and press through a potato ricer. Set aside. When meat has finished cooking, mix in the riced potatoes and let cool.

Roll out half of the pie dough into three 9-inch (23 cm) rounds and place in the bottom of the pie plates. Divide meat mixture between the 3 pies. Use the remaining pie dough to create 3 more 9-inch (23 cm) rounds and cover each pie. Crimp edges and cut a steam vent in the centres of the pies. Bake for 35 to 40 minutes, or until the crusts are golden. Brush crusts with butter to give them a golden sheen.

If freezing meat pies, do not bake them. When you are ready to use, thaw and bake.

MAKES THREE 9-INCH (23 CM) PIES

1 Tbsp (15 mL) lard
½ cup (125 mL) finely diced onions
1 garlic clove, finely diced
3 lb (1.3 kg) ground pork
1 lb (450 g) ground veal or beef
1 cup (250 mL) beef broth
1 tsp (5 mL) salt
¼ tsp (1 mL) freshly ground pepper
Pinch of allspice
2 cups (500 mL) coarsely chopped peeled potatoes
6 Savoury Pie Dough shells (see page 119)
1 Tbsp (15 mL) melted butter

MEAT LOAF
Pain à la Viande

MAKES 4 SERVINGS

1 lb (450 g) ground beef
½ lb (250 g) ground pork
2 cloves garlic, minced
¼ cup (60 mL) diced green
   onions
½ tsp (2 mL) hot sauce
1 tsp (5 mL) Worcestershire
   sauce
½ cup (125 mL) ketchup
1 tsp (5 mL) salt
1 tsp (5 mL) freshly ground
   pepper
1 tsp (5 mL) dry mustard
1 egg
1 cup (250 mL) rolled oats

KETCHUP SAUCE

1 Tbsp (15 mL) butter
½ cup (125 mL) brown sugar
1 tsp (5 mL) salt
½ cup (125 mL) ketchup
¼ cup (60 mL) white vinegar
1 tsp (5 mL) dry mustard

THERE ARE HUNDREDS of different recipes for meatloaf, some relying on canned soup, some on dried soup mixes, some using bread crumbs or rice, and most incorporating a tomato base. The thing that they all have in common is that they are an inexpensive way to feed a family. My favourite way to eat meatloaf is cold on a sandwich. Don't knock it until you've tried it!

Preheat oven to 350°F (175°C).

Line a loaf pan with parchment paper, leaving an overhang on both ends. These handles will make it easy to remove the loaf from the pan.

In a medium bowl, add beef, pork, garlic, green onions, hot sauce, Worcestershire sauce, ketchup, salt, freshly ground pepper, dry mustard, egg, and rolled oats. Mix all ingredients until well incorporated, then press into the loaf pan. Bake for 40 minutes.

To make the Ketchup Sauce, melt butter a small saucepan, add sugar and salt, and allow caramelizing. Add ketchup, vinegar, and dry mustard and whisk. Set aside.

Remove meatloaf from the oven and drain liquid; top with ketchup sauce and place back in the oven for 15 minutes. Remove from oven and allow to sit for 15 minutes, giving juices time to be absorbed and allowing the loaf to firm up. Grasp the parchment paper and lift the loaf out of the pan onto a cutting board. Slice and serve.

CABBAGE ROLLS
Choux Roulés

MY GRANDMOTHER BARD was well known for her cabbage rolls—they were a definite family favourite—but I must admit that as much as I loved them, I wasn't making them myself very often. I found the process of cooking the cabbage and removing the leaves rather tedious until I tried Napa cabbage. I use it raw as it's very pliable, and once cooked you really can't tell the difference. It saves a lot of time and clean up.

Preheat oven to 350°F (175°C).

Heat oil in a large frying pan and sauté onion and garlic until onion becomes translucent. Add ground beef, beaten eggs, freshly ground pepper, Tabasco, and soy sauce to the pan and sauté until no pink remains in the beef. Remove from heat and add in chives and cooked rice.

Remove 12 leaves from cabbage. Place ¼ cup (60 mL) meat mixture into each leaf, fold both ends, fold in both sides, and place seam side down in a large casserole dish. Continue until all leaves have been used.

In a bowl, whisk together tomato paste, prepared mustard, stewed tomatoes, brown sugar, barbecue sauce, ketchup, and white vinegar until well incorporated; pour into a saucepan and cook over medium heat until sugar is dissolved. Pour over rolls, cover, and bake for 4 hours. Uncover for the last half hour of cooking.

MAKES 12 CABBAGE ROLLS

- 2 Tbsp (30 mL) olive oil
- 1 large onion, minced
- 4 cloves garlic, minced
- 2 lb (900 g) ground beef
- 2 eggs, beaten
- 1 tsp (5 mL) freshly ground pepper
- 1 tsp (5 mL) Tabasco sauce
- 1 Tbsp (15 mL) soy sauce
- ¼ cup (60 mL) chopped chives
- 1 cup (250 mL) cooked rice
- 1 large Napa cabbage
- Two 5.5-oz (155 g) cans tomato paste
- ¼ cup (60 mL) prepared mustard
- One 28-oz (794 g) can stewed tomatoes
- 1 cup (250 mL) brown sugar
- ½ cup (125 mL) barbecue sauce
- 1 cup (250 mL) ketchup
- ½ cup (125 mL) white vinegar

ULTIMATE EGG SALAD SANDWICH
Sandwich aux Oeufs

MAKES 4 SANWICHES

EGG SALAD

6 medium-boiled eggs, peeled
 and chopped
3 Tbsp (45 mL) mayonnaise
1 Tbsp (15 mL) finely diced
 shallots
1 Tbsp (15 mL) finely chopped
 green onion
1 stalk celery, finely diced
2 dashes of hot sauce
Salt to taste
Freshly ground pepper to taste

SANDWICH

4 large lettuce leaves,
 trimmed
6 tsp (30 mL) butter
8 slices of bread of your
 choice (toasted, if desired)
12 tomato slices
12 avocado slices
12 rashers bacon, cooked

MAKING AN EGG sandwich is a relatively simple task, but making the ultimate egg salad sandwich requires you to think outside the box. Be adventurous—reinventing an old favourite can be a lot of fun! Our Acadian ancestors may not approve, but I sure do.

In a medium bowl, add eggs, mayonnaise, shallots, green onion, celery, hot sauce, salt, and freshly ground pepper. Combine and refrigerate for at least 1 hour before serving to allow the flavours to blend.

To assemble the sandwich, place lettuce on a buttered slice of bread and top with egg salad, tomato, avocado, bacon, and a second bread slice. Cut into your favourite shape—halved or quartered—and serve.

COUNTRY HAM WITH MUSTARD AND MOLASSES
Jambon du Pays à la Moutarde et la Mélasse

THERE ARE SO many ways to prepare baked ham. Early on in my days as a Chef, we would do the classic ham covered with pineapple rings. We anchored the pineapple with whole cloves and placed a red maraschino cherry in the centre of each ring. It was served with a raisin sauce and we all thought that it was an absolute show stopper! The recipe below is a family favourite.

Preheat oven to 350°F (175°C).

In a large roasting pan, place ham with the bone facing up. Use a paring knife to score the skin of the ham, pour mustard overtop, and massage it into all the crevices. Pour molasses on top, allowing it to run down the sides of the ham. Add water to the bottom of the roasting pan and add in carrots and onion. Sprinkle with freshly ground pepper.

Roast ham for 3 hours, rotating the pan every hour or so and using a turkey baster to baste the ham with pan juices every 30 minutes. Reduce oven temperature to 250°F (120°C) for the final hour.

MAKES 6 TO 8 SERVINGS

5 to 7 lb (2.25 to 3.15 kg) smoked ham (bone in)
1 cup (250 mL) prepared mustard
2 cups (500 mL) molasses
1 cup (250 mL) water
2 carrots, cut into chunks
1 onion, cut into chunks
1 tsp (5 mL) freshly ground pepper

CAJUN RECIPES

RANDY'S JAMBALAYA
Le Jambalaya de Randy
RECIPE BY RANDY MENARD

MAKES 8 SERVINGS

¼ cup (60 mL) vegetable oil

1½ lb (680 g) pork shoulder, cubed

1 lb (450 g) pork sausage, smoked or fresh

2 onions, diced

1 green bell pepper, diced

3 ribs of celery, diced

5 cups (1.25 L) water

4 chicken bouillon cubes

2 Tbsp (30 mL) Cajun seasoning + extra to taste (see page 133)

2 cups (500 mL) uncooked rice, long grain

¼ tsp (1 mL) ground bay leaf

¼ tsp (1 mL) liquid smoke (optional)

ATTORNEY BY DAY and master jambalaya maker in his spare time, Randy Menard is the maestro of this recipe, which he has been known to prepare for events throughout Acadian Cajun County. I must say I have had my fair share of jambalaya over the years, but my buddy Randy's is awesome and I can say I have learned from one of the best. I like it so much that I bought his 15-gallon (60 L) pot, which can make jambalaya for close to 200 people at once!

In a heavy bottomed saucepan, heat oil on high and brown pork shoulder; set aside. In the same pan, brown sausage and set aside. In the same pan again, sauté onions, green pepper, and celery. Once vegetables are sautéed, add the meats back into the saucepan with 1½ cups (375 mL) water. Add chicken bouillon and Cajun seasoning and cook on medium heat until pork is almost tender. Once pork is almost tender, add rice, bay leaf, liquid smoke, and the rest of the water; cook on medium heat until the mixture begins to boil, then lower heat. Taste the liquid to make sure your seasoning is right and adjust it according to taste. Cook uncovered until the liquid is absorbed and you can see rice above the water level. At this point, reduce heat and cover the pot, allowing the jambalaya to cook for 20 minutes; stir occasionally to make sure it is not sticking to bottom of pot. After 20 minutes, shut off heat and let sit for 30 minutes covered, stirring only once midway through that time. After 30 minutes, it is ready to serve.

 When you season your water you will need to over-season it a bit as the rice absorbs some of the flavour.

MR. RAY'S FAMOUS CAJUN GUMBO
Le Gumbo Cajun de M. Ray

RECIPE BY RAY TRAHAN

MAKES 12 TO 14 SERVINGS

Two 5-lb (2.25 kg) chickens, cut into 8 to 10 pieces each

Cajun seasoning (such as Tony Chacherie; see page 133) to taste

2 cups (500 mL) all-purpose flour

1 cup (250 mL) vegetable oil + extra for chicken

1½ gallons (6 L) water

1 tsp (5 mL) ground bay leaf or 2 to 3 leaves

1 tsp (5 mL) minced garlic

5 cups (1.25 L) chopped onions

½ cup (125 mL) cubed pork tasso (seasoned dry meat)

1 lb (450 g) smoked pork sausage, sliced ½ inch (1 cm) thick

Dash of freshly ground pepper (optional)

¼ cup (60 mL) chopped parsley

¼ cup (60 mL) green onion tops

Cooked rice, for serving

RAY TRAHAN: *I remember when the first cool weather arrived in the Acadiana region, every household had gumbo on the menu that night and all the grocery stores knew to expect long lines of shoppers picking up fixings for the traditional meal used to greet the fall/winter season: chicken and sausage gumbo. And the best aroma always came from my house. My mother's roux had the nuttiest and most memorable scent imaginable.*

Season chicken heavily with Cajun seasoning, then refrigerate.

In a cast iron pot (or magnetite pot), mix flour and 1 cup (250 mL) oil and cook over medium-high heat. Stir constantly with a flat-edge wooden spoon, not allowing ingredients to stick or burn. When the roux turns to a medium chocolate-brown colour, remove from burner immediately, stirring to cool completely. (Roux burns easily and must be watched closely; Cajun cooks never turn their back on a pot of simmering roux.)

Fill a large gumbo pot with water and bring to a boil. Add totally cooled roux one large spoon at a time, mixing well with the boiling water. Add ground bay leaf (or leaves) and garlic and continue to boil slightly.

In a separate large pot, brown chicken in batches of 6 to 8 pieces (with room between each), using 2 Tbsp (30 mL) vegetable oil per batch. Transfer chicken pieces to a platter and set aside. When chicken has been browned, sauté onions in the pan drippings. Add a bit of water to deglaze the pot and pour the pan drippings and onions into the boiling roux and water mixture. Cook on medium-high heat for 1 hour. Add tasso and sausage. After 15 minutes, add chicken and cook about 50 minutes or until tender. Add a dash of freshly ground black pepper and additional seasoning, if needed. Add chopped parsley and onion tops. Serve over cooked rice.

 Tradition has been to serve gumbo with sides of warm potato salad or roasted sweet potatoes. Homemade bread completed this beloved and favourite meal of Cajuns.

For this recipe, a good eye is important. If there's not enough roux it will taste like seasoned water. If there's too much roux, it will taste bitter.

The word "gumbo" comes from the Africans who established what is now Acadiana, Louisiana, before the Acadians themselves arrived. The word guingombo describes a vegetable with seeds such as okra, which the Africans used to make soup. Cajuns adopted this soup dish, adding roux with chicken, duck, or seafood, and shortened the name to gumbo.

LOUISIANA CRAWFISH
Étouffé d'Écrevisses de la Louisiane
RECIPE BY RAY TRAHAN

MAKES 4 SERVINGS

1 large onion, chopped
½ green bell pepper, chopped
¾ cup (175 mL) butter
1 or 2 Tbsp (15 to 30 mL)
    all-purpose flour (optional)
2 lb (900 g) crawfish tail
    meat, peeled (or lobster
    meat)
2 green onions, chopped
1 tsp (5 mL) Cajun seasoning
    (see page 133)
Cooked rice, for serving

RAY TRAHAN: *We did not grow up eating crawfish as we know it today. We were only lucky enough to enjoy this unknown delicacy just before harvesting the rice crops our family lived off. When it was time to cut the rice, the water was drained so the combines (large harvesting machines) could enter the land.*

At that time, we would catch the crawfish that came out of the rice paddies, and it was then we savoured just the beginning of what became one of the largest industries in Louisiana. I use three main tools when cooking Cajun food: eyes, nose, and taste buds. Fresh product and the correct amount of appropriate seasoning are also very important.

In a large pot over medium heat, sauté onion and bell pepper in butter until tender. If desired, add flour to the onions while sautéing, to thicken. You may need to add a very small amount of water. Add crawfish tails with juices from the bag (or lobster with juices). Cover and cook for 10 to 15 minutes. Stir once or twice. Add green onion and stir. Season to taste with Cajun seasoning and serve over cooked rice.

CAJUN SEASONING
Assaisonnement Cajun

CAJUNS USE THIS seasoning like we use salt and pepper, with recipes being passed on from generation to generation. Commercially there are over 100 brands available, most of them the same base with variations of certain herbs; some are sweet, some are not. It comes down to personal preference—once you find a brand that you really like, you stick with it.

This is a basic recipe that I love to use as a base and I tend to play with it depending on how I feel. Sometimes I add a local flair with powdered maple sugar, other times I may add oregano.

In a shaker, add salt, white pepper, cayenne pepper, paprika, onion powder, and garlic powder. Mix well and keep in a cool dry place.

The uses for this seasoning are limited only by your imagination. It's fabulous on pork but can also add a kick to popcorn.

MAKES 1 CUP (250 ML)

½ cup (125 mL) salt
2 Tbsp (30 mL) ground white pepper
1 Tbsp (15 mL) cayenne pepper
3 Tbsp (45 mL) sweet paprika
2 Tbsp (30 mL) onion powder
2 Tbsp (30 mL) garlic powder

LAYERED CAJUN FISH COURTBOUILLION

Court Bouillon Étagé de Poisson Cajun

RECIPE BY RAY TRAHAN

MAKES 4 SERVINGS

½ cup (125 mL) butter
1 large onion, chopped, divided
2 lb (900 g) fresh catfish filets (white flaky fish), cut into 2-inch (5 cm) squares, divided
1 tsp (5 mL) Cajun Seasoning (see page 133), divided
1¼ cups (310 mL) tomato sauce
¼ cup (60 mL) chopped parsley or green onion tops
All-purpose flour (optional)
Cooked rice, for serving

RAY TRAHAN: *In my Dad's day, hand fishing was done in the bayous. The Cajun fisherman would walk in the bayou, go underwater, and feel for fish nesting in little channels or tree roots. Other methods such as seining were also used when water was low. The fish were cleaned and cooked over an open fire. Quick, easy, and so delicious. Now this art is almost a lost tradition. Catfish is a fresh local wild fish from the bayous of Louisiana.*

Melt butter in a thick cast iron pot or thick magnolite pot. Add thin layer of chopped onion, a layer of fish, then another layer of chopped onions and ½ tsp (2 mL) Cajun seasoning. Add a second layer of fish with the last of chopped onions and the remaining ½ tsp (2 mL) Cajun seasoning on top. After adding the last layer of onions, pour tomato sauce over all ingredients and cover the pot.

Cook over low heat and twist the handle to rotate the pot clockwise, then counter-clockwise, so that the fish slides in pot without stirring. (Stirring the pot will break the fish apart.) If thickening is needed, add a little diluted all-purpose flour or dilute 1 tsp (5 mL) roux in a small amount of water and add to the mixture. You will achieve a slightly different flavour with roux; however, it is still very good.

Cook 20 to 30 minutes then add parsley or green onions on top. Add more Cajun seasoning if needed and serve over cooked rice.

 Rice was used in most Cajun dishes; it was the staple of Cajun livelihood. It's still an important crop today.

CRACKLIN

Gratton (CAJUN)
Croustilles de Porc (FRENCH)

MAKES 4 SERVINGS

1 gallon (4 L) cooking oil or
    pork lard
5 to 10 lb (2.25 to 4.5 kg) pork
    belly skins, cut into 1-inch
    (2.5 cm) squares
Cold water

MANY PEOPLE AREN'T aware that the Acadians became known as Cajuns. It's very fascinating and if you have any Acadian roots, I highly recommend a trip to Louisiana to visit your Cajun cousins! Cracklin is sold everywhere, and once you have had your first one you will want to eat the whole bag. Usually cracklin is served in a brown paper bag to absorb some of the fat. When it comes to seasoning, it is based on your tastes. Sort of like ketchup on fries, some love a lot and some don't.

Heat oil to 300°F (150°C) in a very large cast iron pot. Add pork skins and stir. (If skins stick to the pot then oil is not hot enough.) Stir often (if not constantly) for about 1 hour with the temperature remaining around 250 to 300°F (120 to 150°C). After about 1 hour, or when skins are the colour of peanut butter, turn heat off and let sit until the temperature drops to 200°F (95°C) or all skins are submerged in oil. Turn heat back to high. Once oil starts to bubble hard again and skins are floating, sprinkle cold water on skins several times while stirring for a couple of minutes. You will see skins start to blister. Dish skins out and sprinkle with salt or Cajun seasoning to taste.

You will find pork belly skins at your butcher.

It might take several batches before you succeed with the recipe—it is always best to watch someone first.

You can cook larger batches, depending on the pot size.

For each 5 lb (2.25 kg) batch of pork skin, the yield will be about 1 lb (450 g) of cracklin.

CLASSIC CAJUN WHITE BOUDIN
Boudin Classique Cajun

IN CAJUN COUNTRY, boudin is made with pork, rice, and liver and sold in gas stations in every single parish, similar to how hot dogs are sold in gas stations in Canada. Everyone eats boudin and everyone has their favourites. On my last visit, I asked many people where their favourite boudin came from and they all had a different answer. For me the verdict is still out, but having had the opportunity to work with the team from Nunu's grocery store (a local grocery chain in Louisiana) each year, I can say firsthand that theirs is hard to beat. My bucket list includes being a judge at the Louisiana Boudin Festival!

Fill a stock pot with water and add pork butt, onions, bell pepper, and pork liver. Bring to a rolling boil then reduce to a simmer for 1 hour and 30 minutes, adding more water as needed. While the meat boils, cook rice as prescribed on the packaging, then set aside.

Use a slotted spoon to remove vegetables, pork, and liver from the stock and pass them through a meat grinder. Add meat and vegetables back into the stock. Cook until most of the liquid has evaporated, stock should measure around 2½ cups (625 mL). Stir in the cooked rice, chopped green onions, and garlic; add pepper and Cajun seasoning to taste.

Tie a knot at the end of the casing. Stuff rice-and-meat mixture into sausage casing using a sausage stuffer. Twist every 6 inches (15 cm) to make individual links, and tie a knot to close off the casing. Refrigerate for a minimum of 24 hours. To prepare boudin, cook in simmering water for 12 minutes. Remove from water and serve.

You won't need the full 20 feet (6.1 m) of casing, this is just how it is sold.

MAKES 12 SAUSAGE LINKS

8 cups (2 L) water + more as needed
2 to 3 lb (0.9 to 1.3 kg) pork butt roast, cut into 1-inch (2.5 cm) pieces
2 medium onions, diced fine
1 green bell pepper, diced fine
8 oz (235 g) fresh pork liver, chopped
3 cups (750 mL) cooked rice
1 bunch green onions, tops only
2 cloves garlic, finely chopped
Freshly ground black pepper to taste
Cajun seasoning (see page 133) to taste
20 ft (6.1 m) sausage casing (see note)

WILLIAM'S SAUCE PICANTE

Sauce Piquante de William

RECIPE BY CHEF WILLIAM MENARD, GATOR
COVE RESTAURANT, LAFAYETTE

MAKES 6 TO 8 SERVINGS

1 cup (250 mL) canola oil,
    divided
One 2½-lb (1.15 kg) chicken,
    cut into pieces
4 cups (1 L) finely diced trinity
    (see note)
½ cup (125 mL) all-purpose
    flour
1 cup (250 mL) Rotel toma-
    toes (tomato chili pepper
    blend)
¾ cup (175 mL) tomato sauce
3½ cups (875 mL) diced
    tomatoes
6 cups (1.5 L) chicken stock
2 Tbsp (30 mL) minced garlic
1½ tsp (7 mL) ground bay leaf
Freshly ground black pepper
    to taste
2 Tbsp (30 mL) chopped fresh
    parsley
2 Tbsp (30 mL) chopped
    green onions
Cooked rice, for serving

ACADIAN CAJUN INGENUITY often came into play when adapting to available local ingredients—some that were quite foreign, such as a turtle. As a result, Cajuns came up with a way to make turtle flavourful by creating a sauce picante (spicy sauce). Of course, these days most turtles are protected and chicken is used in its place.

Heat ½ cup (125 mL) oil in a large heavy bottomed pot on medium heat. Sear chicken pieces for 3 to 4 minutes per side, remove from pot, and set aside.

Heat remainder of the oil in the same pot, add trinity and sauté until onions turn translucent. Add flour, stir well, and cook on low for about 15 minutes (do not brown). Add Rotel tomatoes, tomato sauce, and diced tomatoes; mix well and simmer for 30 minutes. Add chicken stock, garlic, and ground bay leaf; mix well and simmer for 2 hours. Add chicken pieces and continue to cook for an additional 30 minutes or until chicken is cooked through. Add freshly ground pepper for seasoning and garnish with fresh parsley and green onions. Serve on rice.

 Trinity is very similar to what we refer to as a mirepoix, but while a mirepoix is an equal combination of finely diced onion, celery, and carrot, trinity replaces the carrot with green bell pepper.

If Rotel tomatoes aren't available, substitute with regular canned tomatoes and 2 tsp (10 mL) chili peppers.

PECAN BANANA NUT BREAD

Pain aux Bananes et aux Pacanes

RECIPE BY BRENDA TRAHAN

MAKES 6 SERVINGS

1 tsp (5 mL) baking soda
½ tsp (2 mL) water
1½ cups (375 mL) all-purpose
  flour
1½ cups (375 mL) white sugar
½ cup (125 mL) vegetable oil
5 tsp (75 mL) sour cream
2 eggs beaten (room
  temperature)
1 tsp (5 mL) vanilla
½ cup (125 mL) roasted
  chopped pecans
2 large or 3 small bananas
  (very ripe), mashed
Icing sugar, for garnish

BRENDA TRAHAN: *As a Cajun child learning to cook and bake from my parents, I was always more interested in baking desserts—steen syrup cake, pudding/fig/blackberry tarts, pecan pralines, and so many French-inspired dishes. I especially liked dishes made with bananas. Soon after leaving home for the hub city of Cajun land, Lafayette, I discovered this easy and delicious Pecan Banana Nut Bread. I am now known for this gift I share with friends and family, which they consider the most unique recipe for pecan banana nut bread. My secret to the wonderful moist nutty flavour is the sour cream and my Cajun touch.*

Preheat oven to 350°F (175°C).

In a cup, dilute the baking soda with ½ tsp (2 mL) water. In a medium bowl, add flour and white sugar. Add but don't stir vegetable oil, sour cream, eggs, baking soda mixture, and vanilla. Fold gently until all dry ingredients are moist.

Brown pecans in the microwave in 1 minute increments—they should be ready after 2 minutes. Fold bananas and pecans into the batter. Pour into a greased or floured loaf pan or muffin tins. Bake for 55 to 60 minutes or until the middle is solid and the sides of the bread leave the sides of the loaf pan. Dust with icing sugar.

ACADIAN CAJUN PEANUT BUTTER PIE

Tarte au Beurre d'Arachide Acadienne Cajun

DURING A RECENT trip to Louisiana I was in Houma (a small bayou town made famous by the show Swamp People) and visited a café called A Bears where I had the best peanut butter pie ever. "Abears" is the Anglicized version of Hebert, which is pronounced "A-bear" in French. Unfortunately, I was not able to get a recipe from Mama Abear, so this is my version. Enjoy!

Place graham crackers in a food processor and pulse to make crumbs. Add brown sugar and melted butter and pulse until all ingredients come together. Press into a glass pie plate. Refrigerate for 1 hour.

In the bowl of a stand mixer, add peanut butter and cream cheese and mix until smooth. Slowly add 1 cup (250 mL) icing sugar until incorporated, add vanilla, and mix until smooth. In a separate bowl, whip cream and remaining ½ cup (125 mL) icing sugar. Gently fold whipped cream into the peanut butter mixture, then pour into the prepared crust. Place back in refrigerator for 30 minutes.

Melt dark chocolate and white chocolate and drizzle over the pie; sprinkle with chopped Turtle chocolates.

MAKES 6 SERVINGS

GRAHAM CRACKER CRUST

2 cups (500 mL) crushed graham crackers
2 Tbsp (30 mL) brown sugar
6 Tbsp (90 mL) butter, melted

FILLING

2 cups (500 mL) smooth peanut butter
One 8-oz (235 g) pkg of cream cheese
1½ cups (375 mL) icing sugar, divided
1 Tbsp (15 mL) vanilla extract
1½ cups (375 mL) heavy cream (35 %)
2 oz (60 g) dark chocolate, broken into pieces (about ¼ cup/60 mL)
2 oz (60 g) white chocolate, broken into pieces (about ¼ cup/60 mL)
½ cup (125 mL) chopped Turtles

RANDY'S WHITE CHOCOLATE AND PEACH BREAD PUDDING

Pouding au Pain au Chocolat Blanc et aux Pêches de Randy

RECIPE BY RANDY MENARD

THIS IS A traditional Acadian bread pudding recipe that has been adapted to incorporate local ingredients with added love (and white chocolate). It is also one of Randy Menard's go-to desserts that I feel connects the Acadian to the Cajun in a big way. Old bread can always be turned into something amazing.

Preheat oven to 275°F (135°C).

In a double boiler on medium, heat cream and add white chocolate. When chocolate mixture is melted, remove from heat. In a separate double boiler, heat milk, sugar, eggs, and egg yolks until warm. Blend egg mixture into the cream-and-chocolate mixture.

Lay sliced peaches on the bottom of a 9- × 13-inch (23 × 32 cm) baking pan. Place bread slices on top, pour half of the liquid mixture over the bread, and let settle for 10 minutes, making sure the bread soaks up all the mixture. Top with the rest of the mixture. Cover with aluminum foil and bake for 1 hour. Remove foil and bake for an additional 15 minutes until the top is golden brown. Let rest for 10 to 15 minutes then flip onto a serving platter.

For the White Chocolate Sauce, melt white chocolate in a double boiler. Remove from heat and mix in heavy cream. Drizzle over the bread pudding.

MAKES 8 SERVINGS

3 cups (750 mL) cream (35%)
10 oz (285 g) white chocolate, cut into 1-inch (2.5 cm) pieces
1 cup (250 mL) milk
½ cup (125 mL) sugar
2 eggs, beaten lightly
8 egg yolks, beaten lightly
6 peaches, peeled, pitted, and cut into slices
1 loaf white French bread, sliced into ¼-inch (0.5 cm) pieces and dried out in a warm oven
2 Tbsp (30 mL) chocolate shavings, for garnish

WHITE CHOCOLATE SAUCE

8 oz (235 g) white chocolate
⅓ cup (80 mL) cream (35%)

CAJUN PRALINES
Pralines Cajun

MAKES 30 TO 40 PRALINES

2 cups (500 mL) white sugar
1 cup (250 mL) light brown
    sugar (firmly packed)
½ cup (125 mL) butter
1 cup (250 mL) milk (3.5%)
2 Tbsp (30 mL) white corn
    syrup
4 cups (1 L) pecan halves
1 tsp (5 mL) vanilla

I MET A wonderful couple on my first trip to Louisiana who have been influential in preserving the Acadian way of life, and I'm proud to call them friends. "Mr." Ray Trahan and his wife Brenda introduced me to this recipe. Brenda added this note to the bottom of the recipe: "Avoid making if raining or humid. Is it ever humid in Canada?"

In a medium pot, combine white and brown sugars, butter, milk, corn syrup, and pecans. Cook about 20 minutes or less on a medium heat until mixture comes to a boil. Continue cooking until mixture begins to thicken, stirring occasionally. Test for doneness by adding a small drop of the mixture to cold water. When the drop has cooled in the water, remove it and try to make a small ball that stays together between your fingers—it may take 2 or 3 tests. When ready, remove from heat, add vanilla, and stir until mixture begins to lose its gloss.

Drop mixture by tablespoonfuls onto wax paper or foil. Work fast, keeping the pot over a warm surface if it seems to harden too fast. Works best if you have someone slowing stirring the mixture while you spoon the candies out. Let pralines cool before removing.

 If you have a candy thermometer, the temperature should rise to 250°F (120°C).

FRENCH-ACADIAN FUSION

BEEF BOURGUIGNON
Bœuf Bourguignon

MAKES 4 TO 6 SERVINGS

3 Tbsp (45 mL) butter + more
   as needed
3 lb (1.3 kg) stewing beef, cut
   into 1-inch (2.5 cm) cubes
¼ cup (60 mL) all-purpose
   flour
3 cloves garlic
1 medium onion, finely diced
1 Tbsp (15 mL) tomato paste
1 tsp (5 mL) salt
½ tsp (2 mL) freshly ground
   pepper
1½ cups (375 mL) dry red
   wine
4 cups (1 L) beef broth
1 bay leaf
4 oz (115 g) diced uncooked
   lardons
1½ cups (375 mL) peeled
   white pearl onions
1 cup (250 mL) quartered
   button mushrooms
½ cup (125 mL) finely
   chopped fresh parsley

BRAISING BEEF IS a technique that has been around for generations. The French classic bœuf bourguignon is a recipe that I learned early on in culinary school, and I was extremely proud of myself when I realized that bœuf bourguignon was just the Acadian stew we grew up on but with a fancy name! Leave it to the French to give something a classy name and sell it in high end restaurants! Vive la France!

Preheat oven to 350°F (175°C).

Melt butter in a large Dutch oven. Dredge beef in flour and brown in batches, being mindful not to overcrowd the pan. Add more butter as needed. Remove beef and sauté garlic and onion. Return beef to pot and add tomato paste, salt, and freshly ground pepper. Deglaze with red wine, scraping up all the browned bits from bottom of the pot. Add beef broth and bay leaf. Cover and bring to a boil; allow to boil for 5 minutes. Place the Dutch oven in the oven for 1 hour and 40 minutes, then uncover and continue cooking for 45 minutes.

In a medium pan, sauté lardons, pearl onions, and mushrooms and set aside. When the bourguignon has finished cooking, gently incorporate the mushroom mixture. Garnish with fresh parsley.

 This dish is often served with rice or pasta.

CHICKEN LIVER PÂTÉ
Pâté de Foie de Poulet

MAKES 2 CUPS (500 ML)

2 Tbsp (30 mL) butter
¼ cup (60 mL) finely diced shallots
1 garlic clove, minced
¾ lb (340 g) chicken livers, cut in half
8 oz (235 g) cream cheese, softened
¾ cup (175 mL) diced cooked chicken thighs
¼ cup (60 mL) scotch
1 tsp (5 mL) coarse sea salt
½ tsp (2 mL) freshly ground pepper
1 tsp (5 mL) Herbes de Provence
¼ tsp (1 mL) smoked paprika

THE FRENCH HAVE been known for their pâté de campagne for centuries. I often compare it to our own Creton à la Viande (see page 37). Here I am sharing with you a simplified version that even a basic cook can make and enjoy. It is a combination of several recipes for chicken liver pâté that I have made over the years. Perfect for entertaining!

In a small skillet, melt butter over moderately low heat, then add shallots, garlic, and livers. Cook, stirring, until shallots are translucent and livers have just cooked through, about 5 minutes. Remove from heat and let cool, then pulse in a food processor. Add cream cheese, chicken meat, scotch, sea salt, freshly ground pepper, Herbes de Provence, and paprika; mix until very smooth. Place in a bowl, cover, and refrigerate for 3 hours.

Serve on toast points with pickled onions (see page 108).

For smoother results, you can trim the livers of any visible fat or membranes.

Herbes de Provence may include the following herbs: savory, marjoram, rosemary, thyme, and oregano.

COQ AU VIN

COQ AU VIN is a classic French dish, but one can't miss the fact that it has a lot of similarities to chicken fricot and gumbo from Cajun country. Could it be possible that the French might have been influenced by some of our food customs? This is a simple dish that you can use to impress.

Preheat oven to 350°F (175°C).

Lightly flour chicken and rub Dijon mustard on chicken pieces. In a cast iron roasting pan, melt butter and oil on medium-high heat; add onions and garlic and sear chicken pieces for 3 minutes on each side until golden. Deglaze pot with red wine and beef broth. Add salt, freshly ground pepper, bay leaves, and thyme; mix well, cover, and cook in the oven for 1 hour.

In a frying pan, sauté lardons for a few minutes and add mushrooms, pearl onions, and parsley. Continue to sauté until onions start to soften, then lightly incorporate into the chicken. Let rest for few minutes then serve.

MAKES 4 TO 6 SERVINGS

⅛ cup (0.5 mL) all-purpose flour

One 6- to 7-lb (2.75 to 3.15 kg) whole chicken (bone in, skin on), cut into 8 pieces

1 Tbsp (15 mL) Dijon mustard

1 Tbsp (15 mL) butter

1 Tbsp (15 mL) canola oil

¼ cup (60 mL) finely diced onions

1 clove garlic

1 cup (250 mL) red wine (bold flavoured)

3 cups (750 mL) beef broth

1 tsp (5 mL) sea salt

½ tsp (2 mL) freshly ground pepper

2 bay leaves

1 sprig thyme

2 oz (60 mL) uncooked lardons, cut into ¼-inch (0.5 cm) pieces

1 cup (250 mL) quartered mushrooms

1 cup (250 mL) peeled pearl onions

¼ cup (60 mL) chopped parsley

FRENCH ONION SOUP AU GRATIN
Soupe à l'Oignon Gratinée

CLASSIC FRENCH ONION soup is so delicious and it is best done with local ingredients. This recipe showcases the simple way that Acadians would have adapted to life in France.

Fill a sachet bag with peppercorns, bay leaves, thyme, and sea salt and set aside.

Melt butter in a large heavy bottomed pot. Add onions and sweat until golden brown, about 10 minutes. Add consommé, Kitchen Bouquet, sachet bag, and port; bring to a boil then let simmer for 40 to 45 minutes. Taste and adjust seasoning with salt and freshly ground pepper.

Preheat oven 400°F (200°C). Pour soup into an ovenproof bowl and top with a crouton and a sprinkle of cheese. Bake in the oven until cheese starts to melt and brown on the side of the bowl, about 8 to 10 minutes.

To make homemade croutons use 6 slice of bread, trim to fit the opening of your bowl, brush with butter, and cook in the oven to dry for 3 to 5 minutes per side.

If Kitchen Bouquet is not available, use a browning sauce.

MAKES 6 SERVINGS

1 sachet bag
1 Tbsp (15 mL) black
  peppercorns
2 bay leaves
1½ tsp (7 mL) thyme
1 tsp (5 mL) coarse sea salt
2 Tbsp (30 mL) butter
6 to 8 large onions, julienned
8 cups (2 L) beef consommé
  or beef broth
1 Tbsp (15 mL) Kitchen
  Bouquet browning and
  seasoning sauce
½ cup (125 mL) port
Salt to taste
Freshly ground pepper to taste
6 crouton rounds
1 cup (250 mL) shredded
  Gruyère

FRENCH TOAST
Pain Doré

MAKES 4 SERVINGS

6 eggs

1 cup (250 mL) whole milk

½ cup (125 mL) cream (35%)

1 tsp (5 mL) vanilla

1 French baguette, cut on the bias into 12 pieces

2 to 3 Tbsp (30 to 45 mL) butter

¼ cup (60 mL) Peppered Strawberry Jam (see page 159)

½ cup (125 mL) cream (35%), whipped

THIS CLASSIC FRENCH breakfast, served the world over, was the way that the French used up stale bread (as opposed to the bread puddings that were favoured by Acadians). Both dishes use basically the same ingredients, however one is fried while the other is baked.

In a medium bowl, whisk eggs, milk, cream, and vanilla until foaming. Submerge bread pieces in the egg mixture, allowing them to absorb the liquid.

In a large frying pan, melt butter and cook bread on both sides until golden brown; add more butter as needed. Top French toast with Peppered Strawberry Jam and whipped cream.

 You can also sprinkle toast with icing sugar to make it even more enticing.

JAMS, JELLIES, AND PRESERVES

SPICED CRAB APPLES
Pommettes Épicées

FILLS SIX TO EIGHT 8-OZ
(235 ML) JARS

10 lb (4.5 kg) crab apples
10 cups (2.5 L) sugar
5 cups (1.25 mL) cider vinegar
3 Tbsp (45 mL) pickling
    spices, in a cheesecloth bag

CRAB APPLES ARE defined as any apple that is small and, typically in this region, quite sour. There are still orchards around Eastern Canada that grow them, or you may be lucky and find a few trees in the wild. Since they can be very sour, a lot of sugar is required for this recipe, but the finished product is beautiful to eat with poultry or pork.

Wash apples well and prick each of them with a skewer several times. In a large stock pot, add sugar, vinegar, and pickling spices. Add crab apples, cover, and cook on low heat, just barely simmering, for 1½ to 2 hours until apples are tender and translucent.

Remove bag of spices from the pot and pack crab apples into hot sterilized Mason jars. Fill each jar with hot syrup, leaving ½-inch (1 cm) space at the top. Seal immediately.

 To seal jars properly, top with sterilized seals. Add rings and finger tighten. Using tongs, carefully submerge bottles in a pot of boiling water and leave for 30 minutes. Very carefully remove and place on a dishtowel. Leave until lids pop. Store in a cool dry place.

PEPPERED STRAWBERRY JAM
Confiture aux Fraises et au Poivre

WHEN WE WERE younger we would go out with Grand-Mère to pick wild strawberries in the field nearby her home—they were everywhere and had an amazing flavour. We tried to eat as many as we could while picking in the strawberry patch, but only when she was not watching of course! Those strawberries made the best jam. Peppered Strawberry Jam is a play on a recipe I used to do as a Maître d'Hôtel at the old Wandlyn Hotel in Edmundston, New Brunswick.

Melt butter in a large heavy bottomed pot; add sugar and cook into a caramel. Add orange juice and mix well. Add strawberries, crushing some as you stir. Add freshly ground pepper and rum. Once the mixture starts to bubble, reduce heat and simmer for 1 hour. Stir occasionally to avoid sticking. Place jam into sterilized jars and process using the procedure on page 158.

FILLS SIX 8-OZ (235 ML) JARS

½ cup (125 mL) butter
2 cups (500 mL) sugar
2 oranges, juiced
1½ gallons (6 L) fresh
   strawberries
Enough freshly ground pepper
   for 100 turns of a pepper
   mill
½ cup (125 mL) amber rum

PUMPKIN PRESERVE
Confiture à la Citrouille

GOING TO GRAND-MÈRE Bosse's was all about food treats. Sitting on the door step with a bowl of ice cream is one thing, but adding her pumpkin preserves to it was incredible. Today, I can think of many applications for pumpkin preserve in the culinary world—perfect add to a charcuterie board, serve on top of double-cream brie, spread on toasted homemade bread . . . the list goes on.

Cut pumpkin into quarters and scrape out the seeds and wet slimy part. Peel the skin and cut flesh into 1-inch (2.5 cm) cubes, enough to make 4 cups (1 L). Slice the orange horizontally into about 8 slices and cut each slice in half. Set aside.

Place pumpkin and orange pieces in a bowl, cover with water and sugars, and let sit overnight.

Drain liquid into a saucepan, add cloves and cinnamon sticks, and bring to a boil over medium-high heat. Add pumpkin and simmer for 30 to 40 minutes, until pumpkin is soft but still firm.

Remove cloves and cinnamon sticks from the pan, placing 1 cinnamon stick in each jar. Remove pumpkin from the liquid and divide between jars. Place liquid back on the stove; bring to a boil until it reaches a syrupy consistency, about 10 minutes. Fill jars with hot syrup and process following the procedure on page 158.

 If you have any leftover pumpkin, it's very tasty roasted in the oven with olive oil, salt, and pepper.

FILLS FOUR 16-OZ (475 ML) JARS

1 medium pumpkin (see note)
1 orange
1½ cups (375 mL) water
1 cup (250 mL) white sugar
1 cup (250 mL) brown sugar
4 cloves
2 cinnamon sticks, broken in half

GREEN TOMATO CHOW
Ketchup Vert

FILLS TEN TO TWELVE 8-OZ (235 ML) JARS

1¼ gallons (5 L) quartered green tomatoes
10 cups (2.5 L) thinly sliced yellow onions
1 cup (250 mL) pickling salt
2 cups (500 mL) white vinegar
2 cups (500 mL) brown sugar
½ cup (125 mL) pickling spice

GREEN TOMATO CHOW or "chow chow" was something that we ate quite often, but we called it green ketchup *(ketchup vert)*. In the fall, it was the smell of the green tomatoes and onions sitting in the brine that sig-nalled it was time to head back to school. Growing up, chow was served with most meals, but these days it is most often served with fish cakes.

Wash and remove stems from tomatoes and slice. Peel and slice onions. In a very large glass bowl or container, layer tomato slices and onion slices, sprinkling each layer with pickling salt. Cover with a damp cloth and let rest overnight. In the morning, drain liquid by squeezing it through a cheese cloth. In a large heavy bottomed pot, add tomatoes, onions, and vinegar; add water to cover and sprinkle brown sugar and pickling spice overtop. Bring to a boil, reduce, and simmer for 2 hours. Place in sterilized jars and process following the procedure on page 158.

SWEET MUSTARD PICKLES
Cornichons à la Moutarde Douce

TO ME THERE is nothing more satisfying than seeing rows and rows of preserves all lined up, their jewel tones sparkling! It's a combination of the sense that you get from a job well done and that primal instinct when you're providing for family in the face of winter. I think it's pretty much how our Acadian ancestors felt too.

In a large pot, add cauliflower, cucumbers, onions, and pickling salt. Let stand for 1 hour. In a bowl, combine sugar, all-purpose flour, vinegar, mustard powder, turmeric, celery seed, mustard seed, and red pepper. Drain liquid from the vegetable mixture and add sugar mixture to the pot with the remaining vegetables. Bring to a boil then reduce and cook until the mixture is thickened, about 45 to 60 minutes. Place in sterilized jars and process following the procedure on page 158.

FILLS SIX 16-OZ (475 ML) JARS

1 large cauliflower, broken into bite-sized pieces
6 cucumbers, washed and sliced
6 onions, thinly sliced
¼ cup (60 mL) pickling salt
5 cups (1.25 L) sugar
1 cup (250 mL) all-purpose flour
4 cups (1 L) white vinegar
1½ Tbsp (22 mL) dry mustard powder
1½ tsp (7 mL) turmeric
1 tsp (5 mL) celery seed
1 tsp (5 mL) mustard seed
1 red pepper, finely diced

PICKLED BEETS
Betteraves Marinées

MY MOM PICKLED beets each fall and did a fabulous job with them, but unfortunately it is one recipe that I do not have from her. My sister-in-law uses the recipe below and while it is the closest to Mom's I have ever had, it still doesn't taste quite the same. I think that's the way it is sometimes, it has nothing to do with missing ingredients and everything to do with missing the cook.

Remove stems from beets and scrub off any dirt. Place in a large pot, with the largest beets on the bottom and the smallest on top. Cover with cold water and bring to a boil. Cook 30 to 40 minutes until beets are fork tender. Place beets under cold running water and slip skins off. Cut beets into chunks and place into glass jars.

In a large heavy bottomed pot, bring vinegar, water, and brown sugar to a boil; stir to dissolve sugar. Remove from heat and pour carefully over the beets. Add 1 clove to each jar and process following the procedure on page 158.

 It is best to wear rubber gloves when peeling the beets to keep from dying your fingers red.

FILLS TWELVE 16-OZ (475 ML) JARS

15 lb (6.8 kg) beets
9 cups (2.25 L) white vinegar
3 cups (750 mL) water
6 cups (1.5 L) brown sugar
12 whole cloves

PICKLED CARROTS
Carottes Marinées

FILLS SIX TO EIGHT 16-OZ
(475 ML) JARS

5 lb (2.25 kg) fresh carrots,
 cut into batonettes or sticks
6 to 8 sprigs dill weed
6 to 8 cloves garlic
6 cups (1.5 L) white vinegar
¼ cup (60 mL) brown sugar
2 Tbsp (30 mL) pickling spice
2 tsp (10 mL) dill seeds

PICKLED CARROTS ARE one of my favourite vegetables to preserve. They are very versatile—we use them as a garnish for Bloody Caesars, on charcuterie boards, or just as a healthy snack. If you're not a fan of carrots try using the recipe with yellow beans instead.

Tightly pack carrots into sterilized Mason jars. Add a sprig of dill weed and a clove of garlic to each jar.

In a saucepan, add vinegar, brown sugar, pickling spice, and dill seeds; bring to a boil, stirring to dissolve sugar. Once sugar has dissolved, pour hot liquid over the carrots, leaving a ½-inch (1 cm) headspace. Seal and process following the procedure on page 158.

CRAB APPLE JELLY
Gelée de Pommettes

CRAB APPLES CAN be very sour and making jelly from them requires a large amount of sugar, but the finished product is beautiful to eat and goes well with poultry, or smothered on bread with fresh butter. Crab apples are high in pectin, so this is as natural a preserve as you can make. Don't worry—the flavour is so intense, you don't need a lot to enjoy it.

In a large pot over high heat, add crab apples and fill with enough water to cover. Bring to a boil then turn down to a simmer for about 20 minutes, or until the crab apples are mushy. Strain through a jelly bag or cheese cloth overnight, allowing the juice to drip slowly. Do no squeeze the bag or the jelly will become cloudy. This should yield approximately 5 cups (1.25 L) juice.

In a large pot, combine the crab apple juice and vinegar. Bring to a boil and boil for 3 minutes; add sugar slowly and boil for 30 minutes more, or until a quickly chilled teaspoonful has the desired consistency. Pour carefully using a ladle into sterilized Mason jars. Seal while hot following the procedure on page 158.

 You can make your own jelly bag using some strong muslin. For best results make the bag wider at the top and taper to the bottom.

FILLS ABOUT EIGHT 8-OZ (235 ML) JARS

1½ gallons (6 L) crab apples
½ cup (125 mL) white vinegar
5 cups (1.25 L) sugar
Water to cover

SIDE DISHES

SALTED HERBS
Herbes Salées

HERBES SALÉES IS an Acadian staple. It is commonly used for making soups, stews, fish cakes, fricot, and so much more. Before dried herbs and spices became commonplace on pantry shelves, herbes salées was the go-to seasoning. It's simple to prepare, it lasts a long time, it's delicious, and it's versatile.

In a large bowl, mix together onions, chives, chervil, and parsley. In the bottom of a large glass bowl, spread a layer of herbs about 1 inch (2.5 cm) thick, then sprinkle with 1 Tbsp (15 mL) salt; repeat until all herbs are in the bowl.

Cover and refrigerate for 7 to 10 days, drain, and place into sterilized jars. Seal and store in a cool, dark place. Keep refrigerated after opening.

For colour you can add ½ cup (125 mL) finely diced carrots and/or celery leaves to the herb mixture.

The only seasonings available were salt, pepper, and summer savory, as well as nutmeg and cinnamon. Anything else was "exotic."

In Clare, *des petits onions salées* are still a staple today (small green onion tops, chopped and preserved in a salt brine).

FILLS TWO 8-OZ (235 ML) JARS

1 cup (250 mL) finely chopped green onions
1 cup (250 mL) finely chopped fresh chives
1 cup (250 mL) finely chopped fresh chervil
1 cup (250 mL) finely chopped fresh parsley
½ cup (125 mL) coarse salt

DILLED POTATO SALAD
Salade de Pommes de Terre à l'Aneth

MAKES 4 TO 6 SERVINGS

2 lb (900 g) baby potatoes
   (skin on), cut into quarters
½ cup (125 mL) mayonnaise
1 tsp (5 mL) Dijon mustard
¼ cup (60 mL) chopped fresh
   dill
¼ lemon, juiced
½ lime, juiced
6 hard-boiled eggs, peeled
   and sliced
¼ cup (60 mL) diced celery
2 green onions, diced
½ tsp (2 mL) salt
¼ tsp (1 mL) freshly ground
   pepper

THIS POTATO SALAD is delightfully different. The citrus makes it tantalizingly fresh and the dill makes it a perfect accompaniment to seafood and lobster. I like to use a combination of baby yellow and red potatoes, which gives it a great visual appeal. As they say, we eat with our eyes first.

In a large pot, boil potatoes in salted water until fork tender, about 10 minutes. Drain and cool.

In a different large bowl, mix mayonnaise, Dijon mustard, fresh dill, and lemon and lime juices. Add potatoes, eggs, celery, and green onions and gently toss; season with salt and freshly ground pepper. Refrigerate for 1 hour prior to serving.

MASHED TURNIPS AND CARROTS
Purée de Navets et de Carottes

MAKES 4 SERVINGS

1 large turnip, peeled and
   chunked
Salt to taste
Freshly ground pepper to taste
½ cup + 2 Tbsp (155 mL)
   maple syrup, divided
4 carrots, peeled and chunked
2 Tbsp (30 mL) butter

WHEN I WAS growing up, mashed carrots and turnip were a very common side dish. To this day I can't imagine Christmas dinner without it. It was usually made with brown sugar, but we make ours with maple syrup. The addition of the maple syrup to the cooking water is optional but adds a lovely depth of flavour.

In a medium-sized pot, add turnip, salt, and freshly ground pepper; cover with water and ½ cup (125 mL) maple syrup. Boil turnip for 10 minutes, add carrots, and boil until both vegetables are fork tender, about 10 minutes. Drain and mash. Add remaining maple syrup and butter; mix to incorporate.

YELLOW AND GREEN BEAN STEW
Fricot aux Fèves Jaunes et Vertes

THIS SIDE DISH is specific to the Acadians of the Isle Madame area in Cape Breton, Nova Scotia. A good friend of mine, Justin, convinced his Mom to share this unique Acadian recipe with me—it's very good, easy to make, and a great way to use up all the excess yellow and green beans in season. It was typically served with a pot roast, cod, or salt pork.

Melt 1 Tbsp (15 mL) butter in a large pot on medium heat; add onion and sauté until translucent. Add potatoes and enough water to cover, bring to a boil, and cook potatoes until tender but still firm. Add yellow and green beans, season to taste, and cook for 4 to 5 minutes, until very little liquid remains. Add remaining butter and more salt and serve.

You can also add sliced carrots if you like; add them with the potatoes and add a bit more water to ensure you have enough for the beans.

Depending on your preference, you can leave beans whole or cut them into smaller pieces.

MAKES 4 SERVINGS

2 Tbsp (30 mL) butter, divided
1 onion, diced
3 medium potatoes, peeled and diced
3 to 4 cups (750 to 1000 mL) water
Salt to taste
Freshly ground pepper to taste
4 cups (1 L) yellow beans, trimmed
4 cups (1 L) green beans, trimmed

CHUNKY APPLE SAUCE
Sauce aux Pommes

MAKES 2 CUPS (500 ML)

6 medium apples, peeled,
    cored, and cut into quarters
1 cup (250 mL) water
¾ cup (175 mL) packed brown
    sugar
½ tsp (2 mL) cinnamon
⅛ tsp (0.5 mL) nutmeg

LES POMMES SAUVAGES ("wild apples") continue to grow in many rural areas and were easily available to Acadians, who preserved them in stewed apple sauce. Nowadays, with new varieties popping up everywhere, apple sauce is "new" again. I love serving it with pork, on top of porridge, or just on its own.

In a medium pot, place apples and water, bring to a boil, then reduce heat and simmer for 5 to 10 minutes or until tender, stirring occasionally.

Stir in brown sugar, cinnamon, and nutmeg; return to a boil until sugar dissolves. Serve hot or refrigerate up to 2 weeks.

CRANBERRY SAUCE
Sauce aux Canneberges

DEPENDING ON THE region where you lived cranberries might have been called *pomme de prés,* but in our area we called them *ataka.* Cranberries are ready in the fall of the year and are often used as an accompaniment to chicken or turkey, but try adding cranberries to mayo and using that on your chicken sandwiches. Simple and delicious.

In a medium pot, add cranberries, orange peel, brown sugar, and orange juice. Turn heat to high and bring to a boil, then reduce heat and simmer for 20 minutes. Remove orange peel and bottle the sauce.

You can store this cranberry sauce for 1 to 2 months in a Mason jar in the fridge.

Fresh cranberries are best, but if not available then frozen can be used. For frozen berries, reduce the amount of orange juice by ¼ cup (60 mL) as the berries will contain additional moisture.

FILLS THREE 8-OZ (235 ML) JARS

3 cups (750 mL) fresh cranberries, washed
Peel of 1 orange
1 cup (250 mL) brown sugar
1½ cups (375 mL) orange juice

BREADS AND THINGS

BUTTERMILK CHIVE BISCUITS
Biscuits au Babeurre et à la Ciboulette

MAKES 10 TO 12 BISCUITS

2 Tbsp (30 mL) baking powder
4 cups (1 L) all-purpose flour
2 tsp (10 mL) salt
2 Tbsp (30 mL) finely chopped
 chives
1 cup (250 mL) cold butter
1½ cups (375 mL) buttermilk

TEA BISCUITS WERE quick to make and had a multitude of uses: to accompany a meal, on their own with butter and molasses, as a base for strawberry shortcake . . . but most often they were made simply because the household was low on bread.

Preheat oven to 450°F (230°C).

In a medium bowl, combine baking powder, flour, salt, and chives; cut in cold butter the size of peas, add buttermilk, and mix just to combine. Roll out the dough, cut biscuits into 2-inch (5 cm) rounds, and place on a baking sheet lined with parchment paper. Bake for 18 minutes or until golden brown.

 If you don't like chives, no problem—just leave them out.

PLOYES

MAKES 6 TO 8 PLOYES

1 cup (250 mL) buckwheat
    flour
1 cup (250 mL) all-purpose
    flour
1 Tbsp (15 mL) baking powder
1 tsp (5 mL) salt
1½ cups (375 mL) cold water
½ cup (125 mL) boiling water

PLOYES ARE A traditional Acadian dish that originated in the *L'Acadie des Terres et Forêts* region of New Brunswick, and they are still very popular in this northern region. Because they only had a few ingredients, they were affordable and would give added substance in times when food stores were low on supplies. Ployes were most often served with maple syrup, molasses, or a pork spread called creton (see page 37), and they usually accompanied all three meals.

In a large bowl, mix buckwheat flour, all-purpose flour, baking powder, and salt. Add cold water and mix well; let stand 5 minutes. Add boiling water and mix vigorously; let stand another 5 minutes.

Ladle ¼ cup (60 mL) batter at a time onto a hot, lightly greased skillet (cast iron works best), using a 2-oz (60 g) ladle to pour the batter. Using the back of the ladle, quickly spread batter in a circular motion so that it is quite thin. When the surface is dry and the ploye is covered with holes, it is ready to be removed from the pan. Unlike pancakes, ployes are cooked only on 1 side.

 For best results stir batter between each ploye.

FRIED BREAD
Croix en d'Jeu

FRIED BREAD WAS a big treat on bread making day—it was a very simple dish that was made from extra bread dough set aside to keep both younger and older kids happy. It was fried up and served with whatever was handy, most often butter and molasses.

Start with your basic homemade bread dough. When bread is finished rising and ready to bake, take a piece and flatten with your hand, repeating until all is separated into small discs. In a frying pan, melt lard, drop a quarter of the discs in the lard at a time, and cook dough for 1 to 2 minutes on each side or until golden—watch them closely as they cook very fast.

MAKES 4 SERVINGS

8 oz (235 g) Homemade
 Bread dough (see page 189)
½ cup (125 mL) lard

This is excellent served as a treat but also a great accompaniment to any fricot.

In Newfoundland, they call these toutons, which roughly translates to "old costumes."

SAVOURY PIE DOUGH
Pâte Brisée

**MAKES THREE 9-INCH
(23 CM) CRUSTS**

4 cups (1 L) all-purpose flour
2 cups (500 mL) shortening
1 tsp (5 mL) salt
1¼ cups (310 mL) cold water

SAVOURY PIE DOUGH, better known in the culinary world as *pâte brisée*, is used for making pie crust for savoury dishes such as pot pie, meat pie, or pigs in a blanket—basically anywhere that you would not use a sweet crust. This recipe is a standard recipe that I was taught in culinary school. Thank you Chef Jean Paul Greliler for the continued mentoring all these years.

Sift flour into a large bowl; combine with shortening using a pastry cutter or your hands. In a small bowl, dissolve salt in cold water. Mound flour and shortening and use your hands to incorporate the salted water (run your hands under cold water first to prevent the dough from warming up). Form dough into 3 balls, wrap in wax paper, and refrigerate for at least 1 hour before using.

 You may want to smooth out each ball into a 6-inch (15 cm) disk by hand if you are going to freeze the dough for a future use.

SWEET PIE CRUST
Pâte à Tarte Sucrée

SWEET PIE DOUGH is used for making pie crusts for pies such as blueberry, raisin, lemon, coconut, sugar pie—the list goes on. This recipe is the standard recipe I started out with in culinary school.

In a large bowl, add flour, salt, baking powder, and sugar; mix to combine. Mound flour and, using your hands (or a fork or pastry blender/cutter), rub butter into the flour to resemble a course meal. Add eggs to the flour mixture. Lightly toss with a fork until the moisture is absorbed and dough can be formed into a rough ball. Transfer to a lightly floured surface and gently knead 2 to 3 times. Divide dough in 2 halves and form each half into a 6-inch (15 cm) flat disc. Wrap each half in plastic wrap and refrigerate at least 1 hour, but preferably 24 hours, before using.

I suggest you use a gentle hand with the dough. Do not overwork.

MAKES TWO 9-INCH (23 CM) CRUSTS

2¼ cups (560 mL) all-purpose flour
Pinch of salt
Pinch of baking powder
¾ cup (175 mL) sugar
1 cup (250 mL) butter, softened
3 eggs, beaten

HOMEMADE BREAD
Pain Maison

LIKE EVERY CULTURE, making homemade bread was a weekly chore that brought amazing smells to the neighborhood. Nothing beats homemade bread fresh out of the oven with butter and molasses.

Preheat oven to 400°F (200°C).

In a medium bowl, dissolve sugar and yeast in 1 cup (250 mL) of warm water; let stand for 10 minutes.

Sift flour into a large bowl and add salt. Make a hole in the centre and slowly add the remaining 4 cups (1 L) warm water. Add shortening and stir the mixture until the shortening is completely melted. Add dissolved yeast and mix by hand until a soft dough forms.

Knead dough on a floured surface for about 10 minutes. Form into a ball, place in a greased bowl, cover with a clean cloth, and set in a warm place to rise. When the dough has doubled in size, punch down and cut into 4 equal portions; knead pieces individually and form into loaves. Place dough in greased bread pans, cover, and let rise in a warm spot. When doubled in size, bake for 15 minutes then turn the oven down to 375°F (190°C) and cook for another 45 minutes.

MAKES 4 LOAVES

2 Tbsp (30 mL) sugar
2 Tbsp (30 mL) yeast
5 cups (1.25 L) warm water, divided
12 cups (3 L) all-purpose flour
4 tsp (20 mL) salt
2 Tbsp (30 mL) shortening

TURKEY STUFFING
Farce pour la Dinde

MAKES 6 TO 8 SERVINGS

7 potatoes, peeled and cut
  into chunks
6 chicken hearts
6 chicken gizzards
10 to 12 slices of bread, dried
  (see note)
1 large whole onion, cut into
  quarters
4 cloves of garlic
1 tsp (5 mL) sage
1 Tbsp (15 mL) summer savory
1 tsp (5 mL) salt
½ tsp (2 mL) freshly ground
  pepper
¼ cup (60 mL) cold butter,
  cubed
1 cup (250 mL) canned
  cranberries

IN OUR HOME the stuffing for the turkey at Christmas dinner was taken very seriously. It was always made by my Dad, he would usually start the process on December 23rd. He would begin by laying out the slices of white bread so that they could dry, then all the other ingredients would be shopped for. Lastly came the task of meticulously cleaning and preparing the hand-cranked meat grinder. As kids, it was our job to turn the crank—I can still vividly remember doing this, how important I felt and how I loved being with my Dad. To this day my favourite part of Christmas dinner is the stuffing.

In a medium pot over medium heat, add water and cook potatoes, hearts, and gizzards until potatoes are fork tender; drain and set aside, reserving the cooking liquid. Run bread slices through a meat grinder. In a large bowl, combine onion, potatoes, hearts, gizzards, garlic, sage, summer savory, salt, and freshly ground pepper and run the mixture through the grinder.

Once everything is ground, place the mixture into a second large bowl and finish mixing by hand. If the stuffing seems dry, use a little of the reserved cooking liquid to add moisture. Add cranberries. Place stuffing into a 9- × 13-inch (23 × 33 cm) casserole dish and dot with cold butter. Cover and bake for 1 hour, then remove cover and bake for an additional 30 minutes, or until a crust forms on top.

If you did not have time to dry sliced bread ahead of time, you can use the oven and dry the bread directly on the rack.

There is some debate over the safety of cooking stuffing directly in the cavity of the turkey. The feeling is that bacteria from the raw turkey may contaminate the stuffing. I leave this choice up to the cook, but I do advise that if you are going to place the stuffing directly into the bird that you run cold water through the cavity for several minutes first.

POUTINE À TROUS

MAKES 6 PASTRIES

6 Macintosh or Cortland
    apples, peeled and cored
Savoury Pie Dough (see
    page 186)
½ cup (125 mL) brown sugar
1 tsp (5 mL) cinnamon
Six ¼-inch (0.5 cm) pats of
    cold butter + extra, melted,
    for garnish

ACADIANS FROM ALL regions made this recipe. Considered an upper-class dish, it was done with either whole apples or cut-up apples depending on where you were from and how your mother felt that day. If the apples were to be cut up, they were peeled and diced and raisins and cranberries were added to the sugar butter mixture. If whole apples were used, they would be peeled and cored, with brown sugar and cinnamon inserted into the centre of each apple before being cooked.

Preheat oven to 425°F (220°C).

In a heavy bottomed pot, add apples, cover with water and bring to a boil. Simmer for 20 minutes then remove apples and cool.

Roll out your pie dough to a ¼-inch (0.5 cm) thickness and cut into six 6-inch (15 cm) circles, placing an apple in the centre of each circle. In a small bowl, combine brown sugar and cinnamon; place the sugar mixture in the centre of each apple, sprinkling any excess sugar on top. Bring pastry up around each apple, leaving the hole on top exposed; add a cube of butter on top of each pastry and bake on a cookie sheet for 20 to 30 minutes until the crust is cooked. Once pastries come out of the oven, brush with melted butter for a shine. Serve hot or cold.

UNEMPLOYMENT PUDDING
Pouding Chômeur

UNEMPLOYMENT PUDDING IS one of the first recipes that I made. It got its unusual name because it was inexpensive to make and very simple to put together, usually with staples that were always in our home. Even the maple syrup would have been a staple and not necessarily a luxury. This recipe was inspired by my sister-in-law Monique's mother. It is simple goodness from the first bite to the very last lick of the spoon.

Preheat oven to 350°F (175°C).

In a saucepan over medium heat, add brown sugar, water, butter, vanilla, and maple syrup; cook until a light syrup forms, about 5 to 6 minutes. Pour into an 8- × 8-inch (20 × 20 cm) glass baking dish.

In a large bowl, whisk together flour, white sugar, and baking powder; whisk in milk until incorporated. Pour batter over the syrup and bake for 35 to 40 minutes, or until the top is golden brown.

MAKES 6 TO 8 SERVINGS

SYRUP

1 cup (250 mL) brown sugar
1 cup (250 mL) boiling water
1 Tbsp (15 mL) butter
½ tsp (2 mL) vanilla
¼ cup (60 mL) maple syrup

BATTER

1 cup (250 mL) all-purpose flour
1 cup (250 mL) white sugar
2 tsp (10 mL) baking powder
¾ cup (175 mL) milk

CREAMY RICE PUDDING
Pouding au Riz Crémeux

MAKES 2 TO 3 SERVINGS

¼ cup (60 mL) uncooked
   long-grain white rice
3 cups (750 mL) milk (3.5%)
1 egg
½ tsp (2 mL) salt
¼ cup (60 mL) sugar
1 tsp (5 mL) vanilla extract
2 Tbsp (30 mL) raisins
½ tsp (2 mL) nutmeg
¼ cup (60 mL) maple syrup

A GOOD RICE pudding recipe is hard to find. Early in my cooking days, I came across this recipe that came from the mother of a waitress named Muriel who worked in our dining room in Bridgewater, Nova Scotia. I have been using it since then. It is easy to make and always very well received!

Rinse rice as per instructions on package. In a double boiler, add rice and milk and cook until soft, about 1 hour. In a small bowl, beat egg, salt, and sugar. Temper egg mixture by adding a few ladles of the rice mixture, then pour all of the egg mixture into the rice mixture. Stir and cook for approximately 1 hour.

Remove pudding from heat and add vanilla and raisins. Pour into individual bowls, sprinkle with nutmeg, and drizzle with maple syrup before serving.

BLUEBERRY BREAD PUDDING
Pouding au Pain et Bleuets

BREAD PUDDING WAS made all over L'Acadie from one end to the other. It was a way for us to use up leftover or stale bread. I was never a fan until I had the pleasure of working with a lady by the name of Jo-Ann Landry at the Pictou Lodge Resort in Nova Scotia. She taught me how to make the best bread pudding ever.

Preheat oven to 350°F (175°C).

Liberally spray a 9- × 13-inch (23 × 33 cm) pan with nonstick spray then coat with white sugar.

In large bowl, add bread followed by eggs, creams, brown sugar, 1½ cups (375 mL) white sugar, vanilla, and maple syrup. Fold once or twice, then set aside.

For the blueberry mixture, place a medium pot over medium heat and add blueberries and ¾ cup (175 mL) white sugar; cook until liquid is released. Mix cornstarch and water together and add to the blueberry mixture; cook slowly to thicken.

Gently fold blueberry mixture into the bread mixture. Press mixture into the prepared pan. Top with chopped pecans. Bake for 1 hour, then reduce temperature to 300°F (150°C) and continue to bake until the centre is springy to touch. Remove from the oven and pour Rum Sauce overtop to serve.

MAKES 8 SERVINGS

BREAD PUDDING

1½ loaves thick toast, cut into 1-inch (2.5 cm) cubes
6 eggs, beaten
2 cups (500 mL) cream (10%)
1 cup (250 mL) cream (35%)
2 cups (500 mL) brown sugar
1½ cups (375 mL) white sugar + extra for the pan
1 Tbsp (15 mL) vanilla
¼ cup (60 mL) maple syrup
½ cup (125 mL) chopped pecans
Rum Sauce (recipe follows)

BLUEBERRY MIXTURE

1½ cups (375 mL) fresh blueberries
¾ cup (175 mL) white sugar
1½ tsp (7 mL) cornstarch
1 Tbsp (15 mL) water

RUM SAUCE

In a double boiler, whisk butter and icing sugar together until dissolved and hot. Whisk egg slowly into the hot sugar and mix until thickened. Do not overcook! Whisk in amber rum.

MAKES 1¾ CUPS (435 ML)

½ cup (125 mL) butter
1 cup (250 mL) icing sugar
1 egg, well beaten
¼ cup (60 mL) amber rum

OLD FASHION JELLY ROLL CAKE
Gâteau Roulé à l'Ancienne

MAKES 6 TO 8 SERVINGS

4 eggs, whites and yolks
    separated
1 cup (250 mL) white sugar,
    divided
¼ cup (60 mL) cold water
1 tsp (5 mL) salt
1 cup (250 mL) all-purpose
    flour
1¼ tsp (6 mL) baking powder
1½ Tbsp (22 mL) cornstarch
1 tsp (5 mL) vanilla extract
Jam of your choice, for filling
Icing sugar, for garnish
    (optional)

GROWING UP, Madame Bechard was the mom of one of my best friends, Alain. Going to her house was always a treat—she was the mom who did interesting desserts, completely different from what the other moms were making, and it was at her house that I was first introduced to a jelly roll. What a day that was! I now make it with my favourite Peppered Strawberry Jam (see page 159), which is a twist on an old fashion jam recipe.

Preheat oven to 350°F (175°C).

In a bowl, beat egg whites and ½ cup (125 mL) white sugar until stiff. Add egg yolks, water, and the remaining white sugar; mix. In a separate bowl, mix together salt, flour, baking powder, and cornstarch. Incorporate both bowls together gradually; add vanilla and mix well. Spread cake mixture on a large baking sheet lined with greased parchment paper.

Bake for about 12 to 14 minutes or until the cake is golden on top. Let cool, spread with jam, and roll. Dust with icing sugar if desired.

APPLE CRISP
Croustade aux Pommes

MAKES 6 TO 8 SERVINGS

1 cup (250 mL) white sugar

2 tsp (10 mL) cinnamon

8 cups (2 L) sliced peeled
  apples

2 cups (500 mL) fresh
  cranberries

2 cups (500 mL) rolled oats

½ tsp (2 mL) salt

1 cup (250 mL) all-purpose
  flour

2 tsp (10 mL) cinnamon

1 cup (250 mL) firmly packed
  brown sugar

1 cup (250 mL) melted butter

FOR CENTURIES MOST Acadian families had an apple tree or two in the back yard and a cold storage area in their cellar, which meant that apples were were available much of the year. This recipe is a great way to use up apples—it doesn't take too much time and the results are delicious.

Preheat oven to 350°F (175°C).

In a medium bowl, combine white sugar and cinnamon then mix in sliced apples and cranberries; place in a well-greased 9- × 13-inch (23 × 33 cm) pan. Using the same bowl, mix together oats, salt, flour, cinnamon, and brown sugar. Add butter and mix well. Spread dry mixture over the apple-and-cranberry mixture. Pat down lightly.

Bake until topping is brown and apples are tender, about 30 to 40 minutes.

OATMEAL COOKIES
Galettes au Gruau

OATMEAL COOKIES ARE a classic cookie loved by all. This is a fine example where the food of one culture gets adopted by another—we have our Scottish neighbours who started to arrive in the late 1700s to thank for this one.

Preheat oven to 375°F (190°C).

In a medium bowl, sift together flour, baking powder, baking soda, and salt. Add oatmeal and stir, then set aside. In a large bowl, beat butter and brown sugar, then add vanilla. Add eggs one at a time; add milk and mix well. Incorporate dry ingredients into wet ones and refrigerate dough for half an hour.

Line baking trays with parchment paper. Using a 1-oz (30 g) scoop, drop chilled dough onto the baking sheets. Bake for 12 to 14 minutes. Remove from oven and cool on baking sheets for 2 to 3 minutes, then transfer to a cooling rack.

 You can add raisins if you like them. Add them after the dry ingredients are incorporated into the wet ingredients.

MAKES 24 COOKIES

2 cups (500 mL) all-purpose
  flour
2 tsp (10 mL) baking powder
1½ tsp (7 mL) baking soda
1 tsp (5 mL) salt
3½ cups (875 mL) rolled oats
1 cup (250 mL) butter
1½ cups (375 mL) well-packed
  brown sugar
2 tsp (10 mL) vanilla extract
2 eggs
¼ cup (60 mL) whole milk
1 cup (250 mL) raisins
  (optional)

SUGAR COOKIES
Biscuits au Sucre

THIS IS A simple but very tasty cookie that has been around for centuries. In our modern world we sometimes get too complicated, so I suggest you try this very easy recipe that will give you cookies that melt in your mouth.

Preheat oven to 350°F (175°C).

In a large bowl, mix together butter and sugar. Add egg, vanilla, salt, baking soda, and flour. Combine until all ingredients are bound together. Using a teaspoon, spoon out some of the batter, roll into a ball, and lay out on a greased cookie sheet; repeat with the remaining batter. Flatten each cookie with the bottom of a glass and bake for 10 to 12 minutes until bottoms are golden brown.

 Alternately, you can roll out the dough and cut into your favourite shapes before placing the cookies on the tray.

MAKES 24 COOKIES

1 cup (250 mL) butter
(or ½ cup/125 mL butter +
½ cup/125 mL shortening)
½ cup (125 mL) sugar
1 egg
1 tsp (5 mL) vanilla
½ tsp (2 mL) salt
½ tsp (2 mL) baking soda
2 cups (500 mL) all-purpose
flour

MOLASSES COOKIES
Biscuits à la Mélasse

THIS CLASSIC GO-TO Acadian treat was always in the cookie jar when I was growing up. I think its popularity was because molasses was both available and affordable and had a very unique taste that we all loved.

Preheat oven to 350°F (175°C).

In a medium bowl, sift together flour, salt, baking soda, ginger, and cinnamon. In a second bowl, beat together shortening, sugar, egg, and molasses. Add dry ingredients to wet in 2 batches and mix until all ingredients are incorporated. Refrigerate dough for half an hour before baking—this will harden the batter and make it easier to roll out.

Roll out cookie dough to about a ¼-inch (0.5 cm) thickness and cut into about eighteen to twenty-four 2-inch (5 cm) circles. Place on a greased cookie sheet, leaving room between each cookie, and bake for 8 to 10 minutes. Let cool for 5 minutes on the cookie sheet.

MAKES 18 TO 24 COOKIES

2¼ cups (560 mL) all-purpose
flour
1 tsp (5 mL) salt
½ tsp (2 mL) baking soda
½ tsp (2 mL) dried ginger
½ tsp (2 mL) cinnamon
⅔ cup (160 mL) shortening
½ cup (125 mL) sugar
1 egg
½ cup (125 mL) molasses

GRANDMA'S JAM JAM COOKIES
Biscuits à la Gelée de Grand-Maman

MAKES ABOUT 24 COOKIES

1 cup (250 mL) butter
1 cup (250 mL) brown sugar
6 Tbsp (90 mL) molasses
2 eggs
3½ cups (875 mL) all-purpose flour
1 tsp (5 mL) baking soda
1 tsp (5 mL) vanilla
1 tsp (5 mL) salt
½ cup (125 mL) raspberry jam (approx.)

THIS RECIPE BRINGS back such great memories for me. My Grand-Mère made these cookies on a regular basis, and when the weather would allow, she would cool them on her windowsill, beckoning us to come for a visit.

Preheat oven to 350°F (175°C).

In a large bowl, combine butter, brown sugar, molasses, and eggs; set aside. In a separate bowl, mix together flour, baking soda, vanilla, and salt. Add dry ingredients to wet ingredients, incorporating well.

Roll dough out on a floured surface to a ¼-inch (0.5 cm) thickness. Cut into forty-eight 3-inch (8 cm) circles and cut 1-inch (2.5 cm) holes in the centres of half of the circles. Place cookies on parchment-lined baking sheets and bake for 9 to 10 minutes.

Allow cookies to cool on baking sheets for 3 to 4 minutes, then remove to cooling racks. Once cooled, spread the cookies without holes with raspberry jam and cover with the cookies with holes.

 Jam jams were usually made with raspberry jam, but this cookie marries well with any variety you have on hand.

BLUEBERRY GRUNT
Croustade aux Bleuets

MAKES 4 TO 6 SERVINGS

FILLING

5 cups (1.25 L) blueberries,
  fresh or frozen
1 cup (250 mL) white sugar
½ cup (125 mL) water
2 tsp (10 mL) lemon juice
2 tsp (10 mL) cornstarch

TOPPING

2 cups (500 mL) all-purpose
  flour
¼ cup (60 mL) brown sugar
2 tsp (10 mL) baking powder
½ tsp (2 mL) salt
2 Tbsp (30 mL) butter, cold
1 cup (250 mL) milk
Cream or ice cream, for
  serving

THIS IS A SIMPLE recipe using only one pot, but the results are amazing. You can make it any time of the year, but it's best in the late summer when fresh blueberries are at their peak.

Preheat oven to 375°F (190°C).

In a large saucepan, add blueberries, white sugar, water, and lemon juice. Heat to a boil, then reduce to a simmer. Remove ½ cup (125 mL) of the juice and mix it with cornstarch thoroughly; return to the saucepan and cook for 10 minutes.

In a medium bowl, add flour, brown sugar, baking powder, and salt; stir to mix. Cut in butter and add milk slowly. Drop batter by spoonfuls into simmering berries. Cover and simmer for 15 minutes without lifting the lid. Serve warm with cream or ice cream.

APPLE CAKE
Gâteau aux Pommes

THIS APPLE CAKE differs from other apple cakes I've come across because the apples are baked into the batter, a feature that helps keep the cake moist for a longer period on time. When I was young this cake was often served plain, but a sweet frosting could be added to the top as well.

Preheat oven to 350°F (175°C).

In a medium bowl, sift together flour, cinnamon, salt, and baking soda. In a separate bowl, combine vanilla, apples, sugar, eggs, and vegetable oil. Incorporate dry ingredients into wet and fold in nuts. Pour batter into a greased 9- × 13-inch (23 × 33 cm) baking dish and bake for 45 to 50 minutes.

MAKES 12 SERVINGS

2 cups (500 mL) all-purpose flour
2 tsp (10 mL) cinnamon
1 tsp (5 mL) salt
1½ tsp (7 mL) baking soda
2 tsp (10 mL) vanilla
4 cups (1 L) diced peeled apples
2 cups (500 mL) sugar
2 eggs, beaten
1 cup (250 mL) vegetable oil
1 cup (250 mL) chopped walnuts or pecans

CHOCOLATE CAKE
Gâteau au Chocolat

WHERE I GREW up in Edmundston in the 60s, this was considered a fancy cake to serve company. The fluffiness and sweetness of the boiled icing is well matched by the richness of the chocolate cake. In our house, it was a battle between my siblings who got to lick the spoon of the boiled icing.

Grease two 9-inch (23 cm) cake pans. In a medium bowl, mix together butter and white sugar. Add eggs and vanilla. In another bowl, mix together flour, unsweetened cocoa, baking soda, baking powder, and salt. In a large measuring cup, combine coffee and buttermilk. Alternate dry ingredients and wet ingredients when adding into the butter/sugar mixture. Pour cake mix into the greased pans. Bake for 30 to 40 minutes or until a toothpick inserted in the middle comes out dry. The recipe is best if you put the Boiled Icing between the 2 layers and on top of the cake.

MAKES 8 TO 10 SERVINGS

1 cup (250 mL) butter, room temperature
2 cups (500 mL) white sugar
2 eggs
2 tsp (10 mL) vanilla
1¾ cups (425 mL) all-purpose flour
¾ cup (175 mL) unsweetened cocoa
2 tsp (10 mL) baking soda
1 tsp (5 mL) baking powder
1 tsp (5 mL) salt
1 cup (250 mL) cold strong-brewed coffee
1½ cups (375 mL) buttermilk
Boiled Icing (recipe follows)

BOILED ICING

In a double boiler over boiling water, add brown sugar and water together, stirring until the sugar is dissolved. Boil without stirring until the syrup forms a soft ball when a small sample is tested in water. While syrup is cooking, whip egg whites into stiff peaks. Pour syrup over the egg whites and beat constantly until the mixture holds its shape when cooled. Add vanilla and apply to the cake.

MAKES 2 CUPS (500 ML)

1¾ cups (425 mL) brown sugar
½ cup (125 mL) water
2 egg whites, whipped
1 tsp (5 mL) vanilla

WILD BLUEBERRY CAKE
Gâteaux aux Bleuets Sauvages

MAKES 6 TO 8 SERVINGS

½ cup (125 mL) butter
¾ cup (175 mL) white sugar
2 eggs
1 tsp (5 mL) vanilla
2 cups (500 mL) all-purpose
    flour + 1 Tbsp (15 mL) for
    tossing with berries
1 Tbsp (15 mL) baking powder
½ tsp (2 mL) salt
½ tsp (2 mL) nutmeg
¼ tsp (1 mL) ground cloves
¾ cup (175 mL) milk (whole)
2 cups (500 mL) frozen wild
    blueberries (or fresh if you
    have them)
Log Cabin Sauce, for serving
    (recipe follows)

NOTHING BEATS THE flavour of the first handful of blueberries in August. I remember going foraging for wild blueberries then coming home and having to clean the leaves and debris and sort the berries. The best went into the freezer and the rest were eaten right away. Obviously, the best ones go into this cake!

Preheat oven to 350°F (175°C).

In a bowl, cream together butter and white sugar, add eggs and vanilla, and beat well. In a separate bowl, sift together 2 cups (500 mL) flour, baking powder, salt, nutmeg, and cloves. Add dry mixture to the egg mixture, alternating with milk until all is well blended. Toss blueberries in 1 Tbsp (15 mL) flour and gently fold in the batter. Pour into a greased 9- × 9-inch (23 × 23 cm) square baking pan. Bake for 1 hour or until a toothpick inserted into centre comes out clean. Serve with Log Cabin Sauce.

LOG CABIN SAUCE

MAKES 1 CUP (250 ML)

2 cups (500 mL) brown sugar
1½ cups (375 mL) water

In a medium-sized heavy bottomed pot, dissolve brown sugar in water and bring to a boil for 1 to 2 minutes; reduce heat and simmer for 5 to 10 minutes. Serve hot on cooled cake.

SUGAR FUDGE
Sucre à la Crème

MAKES 16 PIECES

2 cups (500 mL) brown sugar
2 cups (500 mL) white sugar
1 cup (250 mL) cream (35%)
2 cups (500 mL) evaporated
   milk
¼ tsp (1 mL) salt
2 Tbsp (30 mL) corn syrup
1 tsp (5 mL) vanilla extract
½ cup (125 mL) chopped
   salted peanuts (optional)

MAKING SUGAR FUDGE is very easy if you are focused, but one interruption or turn of the head and you forget to stir—it's gone. This sugar fudge is no exception, but our Acadian moms took the time necessary to make it because it is just so good. Meanwhile, my father was always watching his sugar intake and was convinced that if he added salted peanuts to his sugar fudge it would be better for him. That theory doesn't hold much water, but it does make for really good fudge!

In a heavy bottomed pot on medium heat, mix brown and white sugars, cream, evaporated milk, salt, and corn syrup, cooking for 30 to 45 minutes and stirring constantly. Test for doneness by dropping a small amount of mixture into a glass of water—it is ready when the mixture forms a ball. Once this happens, remove from heat; stir in vanilla and peanuts and pour fudge into a 9- × 9-inch (23 × 23 cm) pan lined with wax paper; cool for 1 hour. Cut into 1½-inch (4 cm) pieces and share.

You can add peanuts like my Dad or you can leave them out. Both taste delicious.

It is very important that you stir constantly so that the fudge does not burn to the bottom of the pot.

If you have a candy thermometer, cook fudge to a temperature of 240 to 245°F (115 to 120°C).

Have a glass of water ready to test the fudge.

CHOCOLATE FUDGE
Fondant au Chocolat

MY SISTER LYNE has been the chocolate and sweet maker in the family for years. She brings all the Christmas baking from Montreal home to Edmundston and it's something we all look forward to! She kindly shared this fudge recipe because she loves her petite frère (me). Early Acadians may not have made chocolate fudge, but they certainly would have had sucre à la crème (see page 214).

Melt butter in a heavy bottomed pot. Add brown sugar and milk and bring to a boil, stirring constantly; cook for 5 minutes then remove from the stove. Add chocolate and stir until melted and well incorporated. Pour mixture into a 9- × 9-inch (23 × 23 cm) greased pan lined with wax paper. Refrigerate for 1 hour. Cut and serve.

 When it comes to the chocolate you can add your choice of milk, dark, or white. Using a chocolate bar that has nuts or fruit pieces added will change the flavour yet again.

MAKES 36 PIECES

½ cup (125 mL) butter
½ cup (125 mL) brown sugar
¾ cup (175 mL) evaporated milk
1 lb (450 g) chocolate bar, broken into pieces (see note)

STRAWBERRY RHUBARB PIE
Tarte aux Fraises et à la Rhubarbe

THIS PIE SPEAKS for itself and needs no introduction. It is served in the early summer when fresh strawberries are in season and rhubarb is ready. The sweetness of the strawberries mixes so well with the sour (but flavourful) taste of the rhubarb.

Preheat oven to 350°F (175°C).

In a bowl, mix all filling ingredients together thoroughly and allow to sit until macerated, about 35 to 40 minutes. In a measuring cup, mix together egg yolk and butter and set aside. Roll out half of the sweet pie crust and lay in a 9-inch (23 cm) pie plate. Pour filling mixture into the pie shell and cover with a second pie crust; crimp edges and cut a hole in the middle to let steam out. Brush crust with egg-and-butter mixture and sprinkle with sugar. Bake pie for 45 to 50 minutes or until crust is golden brown. Remove from oven and cool until set, about 1 hour.

 You may choose to use a lattice pattern, as pictured.

MAKES 6 SERVINGS

FILLING

3 cups (750 mL) strawberries, hulled and sliced
1 cup (250 mL) diced rhubarb
1 cup (250 mL) sugar
½ cup (125 mL) all-purpose flour
Pinch of freshly ground pepper
Pinch of nutmeg

PIE CRUST

1 egg yolk
¼ cup (60 mL) melted butter
Sweet Pie Crust (see page 187)
1 Tbsp (15 mL) sugar

SUGAR PIE
Tarte au Sucre

MAKES 6 SERVINGS

2 cups (500 mL) brown sugar
3 Tbsp (45 mL) all-purpose
    flour
Pinch of salt
2 eggs yolks
1½ cups (375 mL) evaporated
    milk
Sweet Pie Crust (see page 187)
¼ cup (60 mL) diced cold
    butter

SUGAR PIE WAS introduced by Quebec trappers into the northern New Brunswick area, and it proceeded to make its way over to L'Acadie because it was so simple and uses ingredients that were available everywhere. The secret is the evaporated milk and lots of brown sugar. I've never had anything quite like sugar pie; it will definitely appeal to those who have a sweeter than average tooth!

Preheat oven to 350°F (175°C).

In a bowl, mix together brown sugar, flour, and salt; set aside. In a separate bowl, whisk eggs and evaporated milk. Slowly incorporate dry and wet mixtures together until nice and smooth.

Roll out half of the sweet pie crust and place it in a 9-inch (23 cm) round pie plate. Pour filling mixture into the pie shell and incorporate diced cold butter throughout the mixture. Bake for 45 to 50 minutes, until crust starts to brown and mixture is just starting to set. Remove from oven and cool for 10 minutes, then place in refrigerator to cool completely, about 1 to 2 hours.

NUN'S FARTS
Pets-de-Soeur

ONE MIGHT THINK the name of this recipe is an insult to our devoted sisters in the Acadian Catholic world, but really it was a term of endearment. Nun's farts were a way to use up leftover dough when making pies; they made a snack that could be eaten while the pie cooled off and firmed up. As kids, Grandma would let us form the dough into "farts" giving her a much needed break, I'm sure.

Preheat oven to 350°F (175°C).

Roll out pie dough. Mix together the brown sugar and cinnamon and sprinkle over the pie crust. Roll dough like a cinnamon bun and cut into 6 pieces each about 1½ inches (4 cm) thick. Place buns in a pie plate and add a small knob of butter to each. Drizzle evaporated milk over the buns. Bake 25 to 30 minutes until golden brown.

MAKES 6 PASTRIES

1 lb (450 g) Sweet Pie Crust (see page 187)
1 cup (250 mL) brown sugar
2 tsp (10 mL) cinnamon
Six ¼-inch (0.5 cm) knobs of cold butter
¼ cup (60 mL) evaporated milk

MOLASSES CANDY
Tire à la Mélasse

MAKES 20 TO 24 PIECES

2 cups (500 mL) packed
   brown sugar
1 Tbsp (15 mL) butter
2 cups (500 mL) molasses
1 cup (250 mL) warm water
2 Tbsp (30 mL) vinegar
½ tsp (2 mL) baking soda
½ cup (125 mL) salted
   peanuts, chopped

OLD-FASHIONED MOLASSES candy with salted peanuts was a winter treat because we relied on snow to cool it down. My mother would prepare the mixture while my sister and I stood with boots and mittens on, and once the mixture had been poured into the cookie sheet and sprinkled with peanuts we would run outside and place the pan in a snow bank. When it hardened, we would take it inside and slam it on the counter and the candy would shatter. Next, we would wrap the candy pieces in wax paper and place them in the freezer. It was a favourite after-school snack.

In a medium-sized heavy bottomed pot, add brown sugar, butter, molasses, water, and vinegar; bring to a boil, stirring continuously. Drop a tiny bit of the mixture into a glass of cold water—if it forms a ball then the correct temperature has been reached.

Remove from heat and stir in baking soda. Pour mixture in a well-buttered 9- × 13-inch (23 × 33 cm) metal pan. Mix in peanuts and cool rapidly in the freezer (or in the snow). Once cold, break into pieces and wrap in wax paper. Store candy in the freezer.

 Once the baking soda has been added, you can alternatively allow the candy to cool, then stretch and pull, using scissors to cut the taffy into bite-sized pieces.

DATE SQUARES
Carré aux Dattes

GROWING UP, DATES were used a lot in cookies. For example, my Mom used to make a half moon cookie and stuff it with dates (these are sometimes called hand pies). But date squares were by far the most popular use for dates. This recipe and method are from a good friend of mine, Dorothy, who in my opinion makes the best date squares I have ever had.

Preheat oven to 350°F (175°C).

In a saucepan, add dates and cover with water; simmer until soft, stirring occasionally. Add a little more water if needed, but not too much. Sprinkle ½ tsp (2 mL) brown sugar over the dates as they are cooking to make them a little sweeter.

In a medium bowl, mix together flour, salt, baking soda, oats, and 2 cups (500 mL) brown sugar. Mix in butter. In a 9- × 13-inch (23 × 33 cm) pan, add half the dry mixture and pat lightly into the bottom; add the dates, then top with the rest of the dry ingredients and pat lightly again. Bake for about 1 hour or until the topping is golden brown.

 This recipe freezes well. You can also warm the squares in the oven at a low temperature and serve with ice cream.

MAKES ABOUT 20 SQUARES

4 cups (1 L) dates, pitted
3 cups (750 mL) all-purpose flour
1 tsp (5 mL) salt
1 tsp (5 mL) baking soda
3 cups (750 mL) oats
2 cups (500 mL) brown sugar + ½ tsp (2 mL) to sprinkle on dates
2 cups (500 mL) butter, softened

GRANDMA'S DONUTS
Beignets de Grand-Maman

MAKES ABOUT 14 DONUTS

2 eggs
1 cup (250 mL) white sugar
1 cup (250 mL) condensed
  milk
1 Tbsp (15 mL) melted butter
3½ cups (875 mL) all-purpose
  flour, sifted
½ tsp (2 mL) nutmeg
2 cups (500 mL) shortening
½ cup (125 mL) icing sugar

BEIGNETS OR DONUTS are served all over the Acadian and Cajun regions. Made famous by Café du Monde in Louisiana, they are now found all over the south.

In a medium bowl, mix together eggs and white sugar, add milk and melted butter, and slowly incorporate flour and nutmeg until it forms a soft dough. Cover dough with a tea towel and let it rest in a cool place for 30 minutes.

Roll out the dough to a ¾-inch (1.5 cm) thickness on a floured surface and cut with a donut cutter. In a heavy bottomed pot, melt shortening and heat to 370°F (190°C), using a thermometer to check.

Fry donuts for 2 minutes, then flip for 1 minute or until golden brown. Don't overcrowd—put 2 to 3 in at a time. Place donuts onto a cookie sheet lined with paper towels and sprinkle with icing sugar.

ACKNOWLEDGMENTS

BASED SOLELY ON what my female friends tell me, I think that writing a cookbook may be like giving birth: it's tremendously difficult at the time, but once you're holding your pride and joy in your hands you forget the pain and hardship and begin excitedly planning for the next one.

Of course, it takes a village to raise a child, and this book wasn't much different. This project would not have been possible without tremendous support from some very important people in my life:

My great friend Linda Duncan, a confident and tremendous source of wisdom who has proved to me that miles do not separate friends. Thank you for encouraging me to write this cookbook and for being my personal editor and manager for the project.

My partner in business and in life, Johanne. Thank you for opening up all parts of our home to the team, for the endless recipe testing, and for helping create the beautiful dishes in our photographs.

My dedicated and talented sous-chef, Lisa Clarke, for doing such an amazing job of looking after me and all that we do.

The crazy talents of my very good friend and photographer Perry Jackson, of Perry Jackson Photography. Working with you is inspirational and just plain fun, thank you my friend!

Special thanks to Joseph Muise for his talented writing, which brought history to life in this book.

Thanks to over *Saltscapes* family for permission to use some of the photography in the book.

I would be remiss if I didn't acknowledge these people who have taught, influenced, and challenged me tremendously in my career to be the best that I can be:

Culinary instructors Guy Delorme and Jean Paul Grellier.

Rick Draper, a mentor, co-worker, and, most importantly, a true friend until the end. My life is richer with you in it.

Janice Ruddock, because if there was ever the definition of a strong woman Janice is it. Your advice has never steered me wrong, thanks for always being in my corner—you're a special one "Pea Two."

And to Graham MacNeil from Maritime Inn and Resorts—the things that I learned from you are too innumerable to list. The day we crossed paths was a game changer in my career. Thank you my friend.

I would like to say thanks last but not least to all of my Chef friends, both professional and non-professional (I believe a Chef is made in the heart not in the classroom) for sharing their recipes and love of Acadian food with me. I shall value your recipes and treasure your friendships.

You are all part of my Acadian village.

A big round of applause to the folks at Experience Acadie for their ongoing support and their belief in me. Their unwavering commitment to preserving the Acadian culture in the Atlantic region has been invaluable in keeping the tradition and practices of this vibrant community at the forefront and ensuring that we stand proud amongst all the cultures that make our region the rich tapestry that it is.

ACADIAN FOOD GLOSSARY

ACADIANS USE MANY unusual and colourful terms to describe their food, some of which may be unfamiliar even to those familiar with the French language. As was common in 17th-century France, Acadians still refer to their meals as *déjeuner* (breakfast), *dîner* (lunch), and *souper* (dinner), and there are many other examples of words that have been preserved in Acadian French that have fallen out of use in France and elsewhere in the French-speaking world, such as *naveaux* for turnips. Acadians also borrowed a number of words from Indigenous languages as well as from English—words such as *madouesse* for porcupine and *bocouite* for buckwheat are examples of this cultural appropriation. Other terms, such as *pommes de pré* (literally meadow or bog apples) for cranberries, were Acadian inventions. Below are some common terms used by Acadians to describe their Acadian cuisine, some of which are typical French words while some are unique to our cuisine.

BAUME mint

BEIGNET doughnut

BEIGNET RÂPÉ potato fritter

BOCOUITE buckwheat

BOUCANÉ smoked

BOUDIN blood pudding

BOUILLON AU MAQUEREAU a variation on fricot made with mackerel

CHAUDRON a cooking pot

CHAUDRÉE chowder

CRÊPES DE LA CHANDELEUR Candlemas pancakes

DÉJEUNER breakfast

DÎNER lunch

ÉPINETTE a traditional spruce beer

ÉPLAN smelt

FAYOTS baked beans

FÈVES À PALETTE string beans

FRICOT soup made from potatoes and meat, fish, or seafood

FRICOT AUX COQUES clam and potato soup

FRICOT AU LIÈVRE hare and potato soup

GALETTES À LA MÉLASSE molasses cookies

GALETTE DES ROIS Twelfth Night cake, traditionally served on the Epiphany (January 6)

GRAINAGE wild berries

HARENG BOUCANÉ smoked herring

HARENG AU VINAIGRE pickled herring

HERBES SALÉES salted herbs, traditionally made with chives, shallots, onion shoots, and wild herbs, used as a seasoning in many dishes

JAMBALAYA a Cajun rice and sausage dish similar to paella, which sometimes includes ham, chicken, or shellfish

LAPIN DES BOIS wild rabbit

MADOUESSE porcupine

MÉLASSE molasses

MORUE SÉCHÉE dried cod

MORUE VARTE salted cod

NAVEAUX turnips

PATATE potato

PÂTÉ À LA RÂPURE another term for râpure (rappie pie)

PÂTÉ À LA VIANDE meat pie, traditionally prepared from pork mixed with other meats

PETIT COCHON a variation of meat pie, where individual portions are enclosed in small half-moon shaped pastries

PLOYES buckwheat pancakes traditionally served alongside the main course, or as a dessert when topped with molasses, sugar, or maple syrup

POISSON fish, traditionally herring or cod

POMMES DE PRÉ cranberries

POUTINES dumplings

POUTINES RÂPÉES potato dumplings, sometimes containing pork meat in the centre

NAULETS sugar cookies in the shape of a small child symbolizing the baby Jesus, traditionally given to children at Christmas

RÂPURE rappie pie, a potato and meat dish with a somewhat gélatinons texture that is baked in the oven

SOUPE DE LA TOUSSAINT All Saints' Day soup, made with cabbage and salt pork

SOUPER dinner, supper

SUCRE DU PAYS maple sugar

TAILLES slices of roasted potato

TAMARIN another term for tire

TIRE soft pulled sugar candy made from maple syrup or molasses, also known as tamarin

TOMPINAMBOUR Jerusalem artichoke, a wild tuber

BIBLIOGRAPHY

Arsenault, Bona. *History of the Acadians.* Lemeac, 1978.

Arsenault, Georges. *Acadian Christmas Traditions.* Trans. Sally Ross. Acorn Press, 2007.

Arsenault, Georges. *Acadian Traditions on Candlemas Day: Candles, Pancakes, and House Visits.* Acorn Press, 2012.

Bennett, Wayne. *La Cuisine Acadienne.* Nimbus Publishing, 1991.

Boudreau, Marielle and Melvan Gallant. *La Cuisine Traditionelle Acadienne.* Les Éditions d'Acadie, 1980.

Chiasson, Anselme. *History and Acadian Traditions of Chéticamp.* Breakwater Books, 1985.

Cormier-Boudreau, Marielle and Melvin Gallant. *A Taste of Acadie.* Trans. Ernest Bauer. Goose Lane Editions, 1991.

Daigle, Jean (ed.). *The Acadians of the Maritimes: Thematic Studies.* Centre d'études acadiennes, 1982.

Deveau, J. Alphonse. *Two Beginnings: A Brief Acadian History.* Lescarbot Press, 1980.

Garnot, Benoît. *La Culture Matérielle en France aux XVIe, XVIIe et XVIIIe Siècles.* Ophrys, 1995.

Griffiths, N. E. S. *L'Acadie de 1686 à 1784: Contexte d'une Histoire.* Trans. Kathryn Hamer. Éditions d'Acadie, 1997.

Hodson, Christopher. *The Acadian Diaspora: An Eighteenth-Century History.* Oxford University Press, 2012.

Jonah, Anne Marie Lane and Chantal Véchambre. *French Taste in Atlantic Canada.* Cape Breton University Press, 2012.

Kennedy, Gregory M. W. *Something of a Peasant Paradise? Comparing Rural Societies in Acadie and the Loudunais, 1604–1755.* McGill-Queen's University Press, 2014.

Laxer, James. *The Acadians: In Search of a Homeland.* Doubleday Canada, 2006.

Le Bois, Ruby (ed.). *Cajun & Creole: 50 Classic Recipes.* Southwater, 2007.

Link, Donald. *Real Cajun.* Clarkson Potter Publishers, 2009.

Nightingale, Marie. *Out of Old Nova Scotia Kitchens.* Nimbus Publishing, 2012.

Ross, Sally. *The Acadians of Nova Scotia Past and Present.* Nimbus Publishing, 1992.

Rushton, William Faulkner. *The Cajuns: From Acadia to Louisiana.* Farrar Straus Giroux, 1979.

Sheldon Johns, Pamela. *Cucina Povera: Tuscan Peasant Cooking.* Andrews McMeel Publishing, 2011.

WEBSITES

2014 World Acadian Congress.
http://cma2014.com/en/

"Acadia: Lifestyles in the Days of our Ancestors." Virtual Museum of Canada. Village Historique Acadien Province of
    New Brunswick, 2003.
http://www.virtualmuseum.ca/Exhibitions/Acadie/exposition_e.html

"Examples of Acadian Words." Acadian & French Canadian Ancestral Home.
http://www.acadian-home.org/acadian-words

"French Language in Canada." The Canadian Encyclopedia. Historica Canada, 2015.
http://www.thecanadianencyclopedia.ca/en/article/french-language/

"Historical Background." An Acadian Parish Reborn. Nova Scotia Archives / Argyle Township Court House Archives.
https://novascotia.ca/archives/acadian/reborn/background.asp

"History of Acadia." The Canadian Encyclopedia. Historica Canada, 2015.
http://www.thecanadianencyclopedia.ca/en/article/history-of-acadia/

"Les Acadianismes: Le Monde Acadien et Son Reflet et les Particularités Lexicales du Français Acadien." L'aménage-
    ment Linguistique dans le Monde. Université Laval, 2015.
http://www.axl.cefan.ulaval.ca/francophonie/Acadianismes

"Meat Pie." Tourism New Brunswick.
http://www.tourismnewbrunswick.ca/See/FoodAndDrink/Recipes/MeatPie

"Melanson Settlement National Historic Site – Interview with an Historian." Parks Canada, 2011.
http://www.pc.gc.ca/eng/lhn-nhs/ns/melanson/natcul/Dunn

"The Acadians – Timeline." CBC.
http://www.cbc.ca/acadian/timeline.html

"The Ploye." Tourism New Brunswick.
http://www.tourismnewbrunswick.ca/See/FoodAndDrink/Recipes/ThePloye

"Traditions de Noël en Acadie." Encyclopédie du Patrimoine Culturel de l'Amérique Française, 2007.
http://www.ameriquefrancaise.org/fr/article-302/Traditions_de_Noël_en_Acadie

RECIPE INDEX